INTRODUCING

HTML 5

New Riders

VOICES THAT MATTER™

BRUCE LAWSON
REMY SHARP

Introducing HTML5

Bruce Lawson and Remy Sharp

New Riders
1249 Eighth Street
Berkeley, CA 94710
510/524-2178
510/524-2221 (fax)

Find us on the Web at: www.newriders.com
To report errors, please send a note to errata@peachpit.com

New Riders is an imprint of Peachpit, a division of Pearson Education

Project Editor: Michael J. Nolan
Development Editor: Jeff Riley/Box Twelve Communications
Technical Editors: Patrick H. Lauke (www.splintered.co.uk),
Robert Nyman (www.robertnyman.com)
Production Editor: Cory Borman
Copyeditor: Doug Adrianson
Proofreader: Darren Meiss
Compositor: Danielle Foster
Indexer: Joy Dean Lee
Back cover author photo: Patrick H. Lauke

ISBN 13: 978-0-321-68729-6
ISBN 10:   0-321-68729-9

9 8 7 6 5 4 3

Printed and bound in the United States of America

ACKNOWLEDGEMENTS

Mega-thanks to co-author-turned-friend Remy Sharp, and friend-turned-ruthless-tech-editor Patrick Lauke: *il miglior fabbro*.

Thanks to the Opera Developer Relations Team, particularly the editor of dev.opera.com, Chris Mills, for allowing me to re-use some materials I wrote for him, Daniel Davis for his description of `<ruby>`, Shwetank Dixit for checking some drafts and David Storey for being so knowledgeable about Web Standards and generously sharing that knowledge. Big shout to former team member Henny Swan for her support and lemon cake. Elsewhere in Opera, the specification team of James Graham, Lachlan Hunt, Philip Jägenstedt, Anne van Kesteren, and Simon Pieters checked chapters and answered 45,763 daft questions with good humour. Nothing in this book is the opinion of Opera Software ASA.

Ian Hickson has also answered many a question, and my fellow HTML5 doctors (**www.html5doctor.com**) have provided much insight and support.

Thanks to Gez Lemon and mighty Steve Faulkner for advice on WAI-ARIA. Thanks to Denis Boudreau, Adrian Higginbotham, Pratik Patel, Gregory J Rosmaita, and Léonie Watson for screen-reader advice.

Terence Eden took the BlackBerry screenshots in Chapter 3, Ross Bruniges let me use a screenshot of his site **http://www.thecssdiv.co.uk/** in Chapter 1 and Jake Smith provided valuable feedback on early drafts of my chapters.

Thanks to Stuart Langridge for drinkage, immoral support and suggesting the working title "HTML5 Utopia". Mr Last Week's creative vituperation provided loadsalaffs. Thanks, whoever you are.

Thanks to John Allsopp, Tantek Çelik, John Foliot, Jeremy Keith, Matt May and Eric Meyer for conversations about the future of markup.

Lastly, but most importantly, thanks to thousands of students, conference attendees and Twitter followers for their questions and feedback.

This book is in memory of my grandmother, Marjorie Whitehead, 8 March 1917–28 April 2010, and dedicated to Nongyaw, Marina and James, without whom life would be monochrome.

—*Bruce Lawson*

Über thanks to Bruce who invited me to co-author this book, without whom I would have spent the early part of 2010 complaining about the weather instead of writing this book. On that note, I'd also like to thank Chris Mills for even recommending me to Bruce.

To Robert Nyman, my technical editor: when I was in need of someone to challenge my JavaScript, I knew that there would always been a Swede at hand. Thank you for making sure my code was as sound as it could be.

Thanks to the local Brighton cafés, Coffee@33 and Cafe Delice, for letting me spend so many hours writing this book and drinking your coffee.

To my local Brighton digital community and new friends who have managed to keep me both sane and insane over the last few years of working alone. Thank you to Danny Hope, Josh Russell and Anna Debenham for being my extended colleagues.

Thank you to Jeremy Keith for letting me rant and rail over HTML5, bounce ideas and encourage me to publish my thoughts. Equally thanks to Jessica for letting us talk tech over beers!

The HTML5 Doctors and Rich Clark in particular for inviting me to contribute—and also to the team for publishing such great material.

To whole #jquery-ot channel for their help when I needed to debug, or voice my frustration over a problem, and being some place I could go rather than having to turn to my cats for JavaScript support.

The #whatwg channel for their help when I had misinterpreted the specification and needed to be put back on the right path.

To all conference organisers that invited me to speak, to the conference goers that came to hear me ramble, to my Twitter followers that have helped answer my questions and helped spur me on to completing this book with Bruce: thank you. I've tried my best with the book, and if there's anything incorrect or out of date: buy the 2nd edition ;-)

Finally to my wife: thank you for all your support, for being my best friend, and for being a badass when I needed you. You've always rocked my world.

This book is dedicated to my unborn baby: I wrote this book while you were being baked in mummy's tummy.

—Remy Sharp

CONTENTS

INTRODUCTION

Welcome to the Remy and Bruce show. We're two developers who have been playing with HTML5 since Christmas 2008— experimenting, participating in the mailing list, and generally trying to help shape the language as well as learn it.

Because we're developers, we're interested in building things. That's why this book concentrates on the problems that HTML5 can solve, rather than an academic investigation of the language. It's worth noting, too, that although Bruce works for Opera Software, which began the proof of concept that eventually led to HTML5, he's not part of the specification team there; his interest is as an author using the language.

Who's this book for?

No knowledge of HTML5 is assumed, but we expect you're an experienced (X)HTML author, familiar with the concepts of semantic markup. It doesn't matter whether you're more familiar with HTML or XHTML doctypes, but you should be happy coding any kind of strict markup.

While you don't need to be a JavaScript ninja, you should have an understanding of the increasingly important role it plays in modern web development, and terms like DOM and API won't make you drop this book in terror and run away.

Still here? Good.

What this book isn't

This book is not a reference book. We don't go through each element or API in a linear fashion, discussing each fully and then moving on. The specification does that job in mind-numbing, tear-jerking, but absolutely essential detail.

What the specification doesn't try to do is teach how to use each element or API or how they work in the context of each other. We'll build up examples, discussing new topics as we go, and return to them later when there are new things to note.

You'll also realise, from the title and the fact that you're comfortably holding this book without requiring a forklift, that this book is not comprehensive. Explaining a specification that needs 900 pages to print (by comparison, the first HTML spec was three pages long) in a medium-sized book would require Tardis-like technology—which would be cool—or microscopic fonts—which wouldn't.

What do we mean by *HTML5*?

This might sound like a silly question, but there is an increasing tendency amongst standards pundits to lump all exciting new web technologies into a box labeled HTML5. So, for example, we've seen SVG (Scalable Vector Graphics) referred to as "one of the HTML5 family of technologies," even though it's an independent W3C *graphics* spec that's 6 years old.

Further confusion arises from the fact that the official W3C spec is something like an amoeba: Bits split off and become their own specifications, such as Web Sockets or Web Storage (albeit from the same Working Group, with the same editors).

So what we mean in this book is "HTML5 and related specifications that came from the WHATWG " (more about this exciting acronym soon). We're also bringing a "plus one" to the party—Geolocation—which has nothing to do with our definition of HTML5, but we include simply for the reason that it's really cool, we're excited about it, and it's part of the New Wave of Exciting Technologies for Making Web Apps.

Who? What? When? Why?
A short history of HTML5

History sections in computer books usually annoy us. You don't need to know about ARPANET or the history of HTTP to understand how to write a new language.

Nonetheless, it's useful to understand how HTML5 came about, because it will help you understand why some aspects of HTML5 are as they are, and hopefully pre-empt (or at least soothe) some of those "WTF? Why did they design it like *that*?" moments.

How HTML5 nearly never was

In 1998, the W3C decided that they would not continue to evolve HTML. The future, they believed (and so did your authors) was XML. So HTML was frozen at version 4.01 and a specification was released called XHTML, which was an XML version of HTML requiring XML syntax rules like quoting attributes, closing some tags while self-closing others, and the like. Two flavours were developed (well, actually three, if you care about HTML Frames, but we hope you don't because they're gone from HTML5). There was XHTML Transitional, which was designed to help people move to the gold standard of XHTML Strict.

This was all tickety-boo—it encouraged a generation of developers (or at least the professional-standard developers) to think about valid, well-structured code. However, work then began on a specification called XHTML 2.0, which was a revolutionary change to the language, in the sense that it broke backwards-compatibility in the cause of becoming much more logical and better-designed.

A small group at Opera, however, was not convinced that XML was the future for all web authors. Those individuals began extracurricular work on a proof-of-concept specification that extended HTML forms without breaking backward-compatibility. That spec eventually became Web Forms 2.0, and was subsequently folded into the HTML5 spec. They were quickly joined by individuals from Mozilla and this group, led by Ian "Hixie" Hickson, continued working on the specification privately with Apple "cheering from the sidelines" in a small group that called itself the WHATWG (Web Hypertext Application Technology Working Group, **www.whatwg.org**). You can see this genesis still in the copyright notice on the WHATWG version of the spec "© Copyright 2004–2009 Apple Computer, Inc., Mozilla Foundation, and Opera Software ASA (note that you are licensed to use, reproduce, and create derivative works)."

Hickson moved from Opera to Google, where he continued to work full-time as editor of HTML5 (then called Web Applications 1.0).

In 2006 the W3C decided that they had perhaps been over-optimistic in expecting the world to move to XML (and, by extension, XHTML 2.0): "It is necessary to evolve HTML incrementally. The attempt to get the world to switch to XML, including quotes around attribute values and slashes in empty tags and namespaces, all at once didn't work." said Tim Berners-Lee (http://dig.csail.mit.edu/breadcrumbs/node/166).

The resurrected HTML Working Group voted to use the WHATWG's Web Applications spec as the basis for the new version of HTML, and thus began a curious process whereby the same spec was developed simultaneously by the W3C (co-chaired by Sam Ruby of IBM and Chris Wilson of Microsoft, and latterly Ruby, Paul Cotton of Microsoft and Maciej Stachowiak of Apple), and the WHATWG, under the continued editorship of Hickson.

The process has been highly unusual in several respects. The first is the extraordinary openness; anyone could join the WHATWG mailing list and contribute to the spec. Every email was read by Hickson or the core WHATWG team (which included such luminaries as the inventor of JavaScript and Mozilla CTO Brendan Eich, Safari and WebKit Architect David Hyatt, and inventor of CSS and Opera CTO Håkon Wium Lie).

In search of the Spec

Because the HTML5 specification is being developed by both the W3C and WHATWG, there are different versions of the spec.

www.w3.org/TR/html5/ is the official W3C snapshot, while http://dev.w3.org/html5/spec/ is the latest editor's draft and liable to change.

For the WHATWG version, go to http://whatwg.org/html5 but beware: this is titled "HTML5 (including next generation additions still in development)" and there are hugely experimental ideas in there such as the `<device>` element. Don't assume that because it's in this document it's implemented anywhere or even completely thought out yet. This spec does, however, have useful annotations about implementation status in different browsers.

There's a one-page version of the complete WHATWG specifications called "Web Applications 1.0" that incorporates everything from the WHATWG at http://www.whatwg.org/specs/web-apps/current-work/complete.html but it might kill your browser as it's massive with many scripts.

Confused? http://wiki.whatwg.org/wiki/FAQ#What_are_the_various_versions_of_the_spec.3F lists and describes these different versions.

Geolocation is not a WHATWG spec and lives at http://www.w3.org/TR/geolocation-API/

Good ideas were implemented and bad ideas rejected, regardless of who the source was or who they represented, or even where those ideas were first mooted. Good ideas were adopted from Twitter, blogs, IRC.

In 2009, the W3C stopped work on XHTML 2.0 and diverted resources to HTML5 and it was clear that HTML5 had won the battle of philosophies: purity of design, even if it breaks backwards-compatibility, versus pragmatism and "not breaking the Web." The fact that the HTML5 working groups consisted of representatives from all the browser vendors was also important. If vendors were unwilling to implement part of the spec (such as Microsoft's unwillingness to implement <dialog>, or Mozilla's opposition to <bb>) it was dropped; Hickson has said "The reality is that the browser vendors have the ultimate veto on everything in the spec, since if they don't implement it, the spec is nothing but a work of fiction" (**http://www.webstandards. org/2009/05/13/interview-with-ian-hickson-editor-of-the-html-5-specification/**). Many participants found this highly distasteful: Browser vendors have hijacked "our Web," they complained with some justification.

It's fair to say that the working relationship between W3C and WHATWG has not been as smooth as it could be. The W3C operates a consensus-based approach, whereas Hickson continued to operate as he had in the WHATWG—as benevolent dictator (and many will snort at our use of the word *benevolent* in this context). It's certainly the case that Hickson had very firm ideas of how the language should be developed.

The philosophies behind HTML5

Behind HTML5 is a series of stated design principles (**http://www.w3.org/TR/html-design-principles**). There are three main aims to HTML5:

- Specifying current browser behaviours that are interoperable

- Defining error handling for the first time

- Evolving the language for easier authoring of web applications

Not breaking existing Web pages

Many of our current methods of developing sites and applications rely on undocumented (or at least unspecified) features incorporated into browsers over time. For example, XMLHttp-Request (XHR) powers untold numbers of Ajax-driven sites. It was invented by Microsoft, and subsequently reverse-engineered and incorporated into all other browsers, but had never been specified as a standard (Anne van Kesteren of Opera finally specified it as part of the WHATWG). Such a vital part of so many sites left entirely to reverse-engineering! So one of the first tasks of HTML5 was to document the undocumented, in order to increase interoperability by leaving less to guesswork for web authors and implementors of browsers.

It was also necessary to unambiguously define how browsers and other user agents should deal with invalid markup. This wasn't a problem in the XML world; XML specifies "draconian error handling" in which the browser is required to stop rendering if it finds an error. One of the major reasons for the rapid ubiquity and success of the Web (in our opinion) was that even bad code had a fighting chance of being rendered by some or all browsers. The barrier to entry to publishing on the Web was democratically low, but each browser was free to decide how to render bad code. Something as simple as
`<b><i>Hello mum!</b></i>`

(note the mismatched closing tags) produces different DOMs in different browsers. Different DOMs can cause the same CSS to have a completely different rendering, and they can make writing JavaScript that runs across browsers much harder than it need be. A consistent DOM is so important to the design of HTML5 that the language itself is defined in terms of the DOM.

> **NOTE** There is an HTML5 spec that deals with just the aspects relevant to web authors, generated automatically from the main source available at http://dev.w3.org/html5/markup/.

In the interests of greater interoperability, it's vital that error handling be identical across browsers, thus generating the exact same DOM even when confronted with broken HTML. In order for that to happen, it was necessary for someone to specify it. As we said, the HTML5 specification is well over 900 pages long if printed out, but only 300 or so of those are of relevance to web authors (that's you and us); the rest of it is for implementors of browsers, telling them *exactly* how to parse markup, even bad markup.

Web applications

An increasing number of sites on the Web are what we'll call web applications; that is, they mimic desktop apps rather than traditional static text-images-links documents that make up the majority of the Web. Examples are online word processors, photo editing tools, mapping sites, etc. Heavily powered by JavaScript, these have pushed HTML 4 to the edge of its capabilities. HTML5 specifies new DOM APIs for drag and drop, server-sent events, drawing, video, and the like. These new interfaces that HTML pages expose to JavaScript via objects in the DOM make it easier to write such applications using tightly specified standards rather than barely documented hacks.

Even more important is the need for an open standard (free to use and free to implement) that can compete with proprietary standards like Adobe Flash or Microsoft Silverlight. Regardless of what your thoughts are on those technologies or companies, we believe that the Web is too vital a platform for society, commerce, and communication to be in the hands of one vendor. How differently would the renaissance have progressed if Caxton held a patent and a monopoly on the manufacture of printing presses?

Don't break the Web

There are exactly umpty-squillion web pages already out there, and it's imperative that they continue to render. So HTML5 is (mostly) a superset of HTML 4 that continues to define how browsers should deal with legacy markup such as <font>, <center>, and other such presentational tags, because millions of web pages use them. But authors should not use them, as they're obsolete. For web authors, semantic markup still rules the day, although each reader will form her own conclusion as to whether HTML5 includes enough semantics, or too many elements.

As a bonus, HTML5's unambiguous parsing rules should ensure that ancient pages will work interoperably, as the HTML5 parser will be used for all HTML documents. (No browser yet ships with an HTML5 parser by default, although at time of writing Firefox has an *experimental* HTML5 parser that can be switched on from about:config by changing the preference html5.enable to true.)

What about XML?

HTML5 is not an XML language (it's not even an SGML language, if that means anything important to you). It *must* be served as text/html. If, however, you need to use XML, there is an XML serialisation called XHTML5. This allows all the same features, but (unsurprisingly) requires a more rigid syntax (if you're used to coding XHTML, this is exactly the same as you already write). It *must* be well-formed XML and it *must* be served with an XML MIME type, even though Internet Explorer 8 and its antecedents can't process it (it offers it for downloading rather than rendering it). Because of this, we are using HTML rather than XHTML syntax in this book.

HTML5 support

HTML5 is moving very fast now, and even though the spec went to first final draft in October 2009, browsers were already implementing HTML5 support (particularly around the APIs) before this date. Equally, HTML5 support is going to continuously increase as the browsers start rolling out the features.

This book has been written between November 2009 and May 2010. We've already amended chapters several times to take into account changes in the specification, which is looking (dare we say it?) pretty stable now. (We will regret writing that, we know!)

Of course, instances where we say "this is only supported in browser X" will rapidly date—which is a good thing.

Let's get our hands dirty

So that's your history lesson, with a bit of philosophy thrown in. It's why HTML5 sometimes willfully disagrees with other specifications—for backwards-compatibility, it often defines what browsers actually do, rather than what an RFC specifies they ought to do. It's why sometimes HTML5 seems like a kludge or a compromise—it is. And if that's the price we have to pay for an interoperable open Web, then your authors say "*viva* pragmatism!"

Got your seatbelt on?

Let's go.

CHAPTER 1

Main structure

Bruce Lawson

ALTHOUGH MUCH OF HTML5 is for making interactive applications, there is a great deal of interest to markup monkeys as well as JavaScript junkies; 28 new elements exist with new semantics that can be used in traditional "static" pages, as well as a swathe of new form controls that can abolish JavaScript form validation altogether.

Let's get straight into the code and begin marking up a typical page with HTML5. We'll transform the current markup structure of <div>s into a more semantic system using new HTML5 structural elements like <nav>, <header>, <footer>, <aside>, and <article>. We'll look at how these work, and how HTML5 documents have an unambiguous outline and are—arguably—more "semantic."

But first things first. We need to open a code editor and enter a DOCTYPE and preliminary information.

The <head>

First, the DOCTYPE:

```
<!doctype html>
```

That's it. No URLs that even the most prolific web authors need to cut and paste. Note that there is no version number. That's all. It's not so much an instruction as an incantation: it's required by browsers that need the presence of a doctype to trigger standards mode, and this string is the shortest string that does this reliably.

Then we need to define the document's character encoding. Not doing so can result in an obscure but real security risk (see **http://code.google.com/p/doctype/wiki/ArticleUtf7**). This should be in the first 512 bytes of the document. Unless you can think of a splendid reason not to use it, we recommend UTF-8 as the character encoding:

```
<!doctype html>
<meta charset=utf-8>
```

Take a look at that `<meta>` tag very carefully. Those who are used to writing XHTML will notice three oddities. The first is that the `<meta>` tag is much shorter than that we have used up until now—we've been used to using `<meta http-equiv= "Content-Type" content="text/html; charset=UTF-8">`. This is still possible, but the shorter way is preferred as it's easier to type and works everywhere already.

You'll also notice that I haven't quoted the attribute `charset="utf-8"`. Neither have I self-closed the tag `<meta charset=utf-8 />`.

HTML5 is not an XML language, so you don't need to do those things. But you can if you prefer. All of these are equally valid HTML5:

```
<META CHARSET=UTF-8>
<META CHARSET=UTF-8 />
<META CHARSET="UTF-8">
<META CHARSET="UTF-8" />
<meta charset=utf-8>
<meta charset=utf-8 />
<meta charset="utf-8">
<meta charset="utf-8" />
<MeTa CHARset=utF-8>
```

Why such appallingly lax syntax? The answer is simple: browsers never cared about XHTML syntax if it was sent as text/html—only the XHTML validator did. Therefore, favouring one form over the other in HTML5 would be entirely arbitrary, and cause pages that didn't follow that format to be invalid, although they would work perfectly in any browser. So HTML5 is agnostic about which you use.

Pick a style and stick with it

Just because you can use any of the aforementioned formats doesn't mean you should mix them all up, however. That would prove a maintenance nightmare, particularly in a large team.

Our advice is pick the style that works for you and stick to it. It doesn't matter which you choose; Remy prefers XHTML syntax while Bruce prefers lowercase, attribute minimisation (so `controls` rather than `controls="controls"`) and only quoting attributes when it's necessary, as in adding two classes to an element, so `<div class=important>` but `<div class="important logged-in"`. You'll see both styles in this book, as we each work as we feel most comfortable and you need to be able to read both.

As a brave new HTML5 author, you're free to choose—but having chosen, keep to it.

While we're on the subject of appallingly lax syntax rules (from an XHTML perspective), let's cheat and, after adding the document title, we'll go straight to the content:

```
<!doctype html>
<meta charset=utf-8>
<title>Interesting blog</title>
<p>Today I drank coffee for breakfast. 14 hours later,
¬ I went to bed.</p>
```

If we validate this exhilarating blog, we find that it validates fine, yet it has no <html> tag, no <head>, and no <body> (**Figure 1.1**).

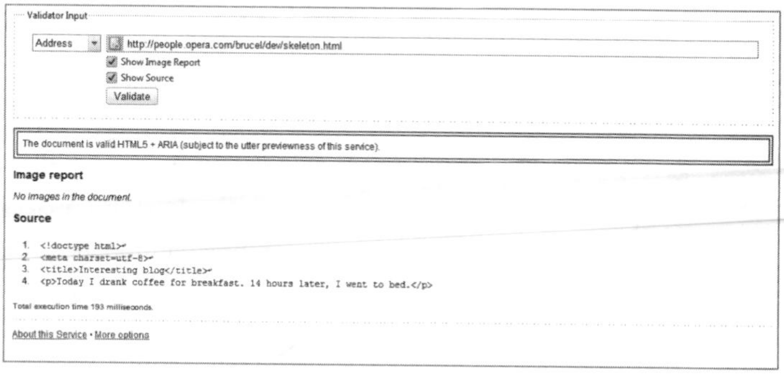

FIGURE 1.1 Shockingly, with no head, body, or html tag, the document validates.

This is perhaps one of those *WTF?* moments I mentioned in the introduction. These three elements are (XHTML authors, are you sitting down?) entirely optional, because browsers assume them anyway. A quick glance under the browser hood with Opera Dragonfly confirms this (**Figure 1.2**).

FIGURE 1.2 Opera Dragonfly debugger shows that browsers add the missing elements.

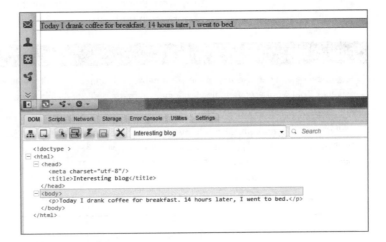

Figure 1.3 shows it using the IE8 developer tools.

FIGURE 1.3 Internet Explorer 8, like all other browsers, adds missing elements in the DOM. (IE seems to swap `<title>` and `<meta>`, however.)

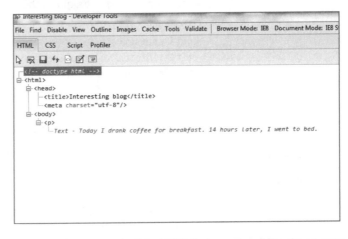

Because browsers do this, HTML5 doesn't require these tags. Nevertheless, omitting these elements from your markup is likely to confuse the heck out of your co-workers. Also, skipping the <html> tag hurts your screen reader users, as that's where you set the primary language of the document:

<html lang=en>

This is important as the word *six*, for example, is pronounced differently depending on whether the language is English or French.

Also, as we'll see later, IE requires the <body> element before it will apply CSS to style new HTML5 elements.

So, in the interest of maintainability, we'll add those optional elements to make what's probably the minimum maintainable HTML5 page:

```
<!doctype html>
<html lang=en>
<head>
<meta charset=utf-8>
<title>Interesting blog</title>
</head>
<body>
<p>Today I drank coffee for breakfast. 14 hours later,
¬I went to bed.</p>
</body>
</html>
```

Does validation matter anymore?

Given that we have such forgiving syntax, we can miss out implied tags like <html>, <head>, and <body>, and—most importantly—because HTML5 defines a consistent DOM for any bad markup, you'll be forgiven for asking yourself if validation actually matters any more. We've asked ourselves the same question.

Our opinion is that validation was always a tool, a means to an end—not a goal in itself.

The goal is semantic markup: ensuring that the elements you choose define the meaning of your content as closely as possible, and don't describe presentation. It's possible to have a perfectly valid page made of nothing other than display tables, divs and spans, which is no semantic use to anyone, Conversely, a single unencoded ampersand can make an excellently-structured semantically-rich web page invalid, but it's still a semantic page.

We think that validation remains useful quality assurance, too. When we lead development teams, we make passing validation a necessary step before any code review, let alone making code live. It's a great way of ensuring that your code really does what you want. After all, browsers may make a consistent DOM from bad markup but it might not be the DOM you want.

Also, HTML5 parsers don't exist yet in production browsers, so ensuring valid pages is absolutely what you should aim for to ensure predictable CSS and JavaScript behaviours.

The validator we use is **http://html5.validator.nu**. We expect to see further developments in validators, such as options to enforce coding choices—so you can choose to be warned for not using XHTML syntax, for example, even though that's not required by the spec.

Using new HTML5 structural elements

In 2004, the editor of the HTML5 spec, Ian Hickson, mined 1 billion web pages via the Google index, looking to see what the "real" web is made of. One of the analyses he subsequently published (**http://code.google.com/webstats/2005-12/classes. html**) was a list of the most popular class names in those HTML documents.

More recently, in 2009 the Opera MAMA crawler (see **http:// devfiles.myopera.com/articles/572/idlist-url.htm**) looked again at class attributes in 2,148,723 randomly chosen URLs and also ids given to elements (which the Google dataset didn't include) in 1,806,424 URLs. See **Table 1.1** and **Table 1.2**.

TABLE 1.1 Class Names

POPULARITY	VALUE	FREQUENCY
1	footer	179,528
2	menu	146,673
3	style1	138,308
4	msonormal	123,374
5	text	122,911
6	content	113,951
7	title	91,957
8	style2	89,851
9	header	89,274
10	copyright	86,979
11	button	81,503
12	main	69,620
13	style3	69,349
14	small	68,995
15	nav	68,634
16	clear	68,571
17	search	59,802
18	style4	56,032
19	logo	48,831
20	body	48,052

TABLE 1.2 ID Names

POPULARITY	VALUE	FREQUENCY
1	footer	288,061
2	content	228,661
3	header	223,726
4	logo	121,352
5	container	119,877
6	main	106,327
7	table1	101,677
8	menu	96,161
9	layer1	93,920
10	autonumber1	77,350
11	search	74,887
12	nav	72,057
13	wrapper	66,730
14	top	66,615
15	table2	57,934
16	layer2	56,823
17	sidebar	52,416
18	image1	48,922
19	banner	44,592
20	navigation	43,664

As we can see, once we remove obviously presentational classes, we're left with a good idea of the structures that authors are trying to use on their pages.

Just as HTML 4 reflects the early Web of scientists and engineers (so there are elements like <kbd>, <samp>, and <var>), HTML5 reflects the Web as it was during its development: 28 elements are new, many of them inspired by the class and id names above, because that's what developers actually build.

So, while we're in a pragmatic rather than philosophical mood, let's actually use them. Here is a sample blog home page marked up as we do in HTML 4 using the semantically neutral <div> element:

```
<div id="header">
 <h1>My interesting life</h1>
</div>
<div id="sidebar">
 <h2>Menu</h2>
 <ul>
  <li><a href="last-week.html">Last week</a></li>
  <li><a href="archive.html">Archives</a></li>
 </ul>
</div>
<div class="post">
 <h2>Yesterday</h2>
 <p>Today I drank coffee for breakfast. 14 hours later,
 ¬I went to bed.</p>
</div>
<div class="post">
 <h2>Tuesday</h2>
 <p>Ran out of coffee, so had orange juice for breakfast.
 ¬It was from concentrate.</p>
</div>
<div id="footer">
 <p><small> This is copyright by Bruce Sharp. Contact me to
 ¬negotiate the movie  rights.</small></p>
</div>
```

By applying some simple CSS to it, we'll style it:

```
#sidebar {float:left; width:20%;}
.post {float:right; width:79%;}
#footer {clear:both;}
```

Diagrammatically, the page looks like **Figure 1.4**.

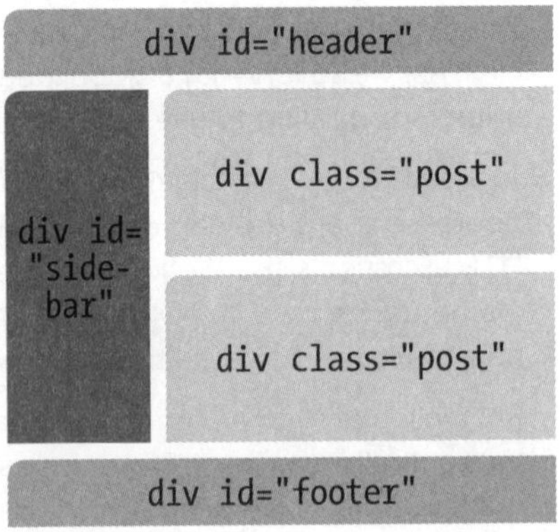

FIGURE 1.4 The HTML 4
structure of our blog.

div id="header"

div class="post"

div id=
"side-
bar"

div class="post"

div id="footer"

While there is nothing at all wrong with this markup (and it'll
continue working perfectly well in the new HTML5 world), most
of the structure is entirely unknown to a browser, as the only
real HTML element we can use for these important page landmarks is the semantically neutral <div> (defined in HTML 4 as
"a generic mechanism for adding structure to documents").

It's possible to imagine a clever browser having a shortcut key
that would jump straight to the page's navigation. The question
is: how would it know what to jump to? Some users use <div
class="menu">, others use class="nav" or class="navigation" or
class="links" or any number of equivalents in languages other
than English. The Opera MAMA tables above suggest that menu,
nav, sidebar, and navigation could all be synonymous.

HTML5 gives us new elements that unambiguously denote landmarks in a page. So, we'll rewrite our page to use some of these
elements:

```
<header>
 <h1>My interesting life</h1>
</header>
<nav>
 <h2>Menu</h2>
 <ul>
  <li><a href="last-week.html">Last week</a></li>
  <li><a href="archive.html">Archives</a></li>
 </ul>
</nav>
<article>
 <h2>Yesterday</h2>
 <p>Today I drank coffee for breakfast. 14 hours later,
 ¬ I went to bed.</p>
</article>
```

```
<article>
 <h2>Tuesday</h2>
 <p>Ran out of coffee, so had orange juice for breakfast.
 ¬It was from concentrate.</p>
</article>

<footer>
 <p><small>This is copyright by Bruce Sharp. Contact me to
 ¬negotiate the movie  rights.</small></p>
</footer>
```

Diagrammatically, the HTML5 version is shown in **Figure 1.5**.

FIGURE 1.5 The HTML5 structure of our blog.

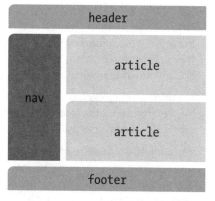

Why oh why is there no <content> element?

It's easy to see how our hypothetical "jump to nav" shortcut key would work, but a more common requirement is to jump straight to the main content area. Some accessibility-minded designers add a "skip links" link at the very top of the page, to allow screen reader users to bypass navigation items. Yet in HTML5 there is no <content> element to jump to, so how would a screen reader (or search engine) know where the main content of a page begins?

Actually, it's simple to determine where it is, using what I call the *Scooby Doo algorithm*. You always know that the person behind the ghost mask will be the sinister janitor of the disused theme park, simply because he's the only person in the episode who isn't Fred, Daphne, Velma, Shaggy, or Scoobs. Similarly, the first piece of content that's not in a <header>, <nav>, <aside>, or <footer> is the beginning of the main content, regardless of whether it's contained in an <article>, a <div>, or whether it is a direct descendent of the <body> element. If you want a belt-and-braces approach, you can use WAI-ARIA and add role=main to whatever element wraps your main content (see Chapter 2 for more on WAI-ARIA).

While it might seem counterintuitive that you can mark up the peripheral areas of a page with their own elements but not the main focus of a page, the content, because it can be easily discovered by excluding those areas, it's best not to add another element; adding elements to the language isn't "free" for browser manufacturers as it adds further complexity to test suites and increases risks of regressions.

Before we look in detail at when to use these new elements, and what they mean, let's first style the basic structures of the page.

Styling HTML5 with CSS

In all but one browser, styling these new elements is pretty simple: you can apply CSS to any arbitrary element, because, as the spec says, CSS "is a style sheet language that allows authors and users to attach style ... to structured documents (e.g., HTML documents and XML applications)" and XML applications can have any elements they want.

Although you can use the new HTML5 elements now, most browsers—even current ones—don't necessarily understand them. They don't do anything special with them and treat them like unknown elements you make up.

Therefore, using CSS we can float <nav>, put borders on <header> and <footer>, and give margins and padding to <article> almost as easily we can with <div>s.

What might surprise readers is that, by default, CSS assumes that elements are display:inline, so if you just set heights and widths to the structural elements as we do <div>s, it won't work properly in the current crop of browsers until we explicitly tell the browser that they are display:block. In current browsers, there is a rudimentary style sheet built into the browser that overrides the default inline styling for those elements we think of as natively block-level (one such style sheet can be found at **http://www.w3.org/TR/CSS2/sample.html**). However, those browsers don't yet have rules to define <header>, <nav>, <footer>, <article> as display:block, so we need to specify this in our CSS. When browsers do include such rules, our line will be harmless but redundant, acting as a useful helper for older browsers, which we all know can linger on well beyond their sell-by dates.

So, to style our HTML5 to match our HTML 4 design, we simply need the styles

```
header, nav, footer, article {display:block;}
nav {float:left; width:20%;}
article {float:right; width:79%;}
footer {clear:both;}
```

And a beautiful HTML5 page is born. Except in one browser.

Styling HTML5 in Internet Explorer

In current versions of Internet Explorer, your page will be unstyled. (Actually, it's worse than that: any new elements are unstyled, but CSS is applied to those HTML 4 elements that IE does support.)

The way to cajole IE into applying CSS to HTML5 is to use JavaScript. Why? This is an inscrutable secret, and if we told you we'd have to kill you. (Actually, we don't know.) If you add the following JavaScript into the head of the page

```
<script>
document.createElement('header');
document.createElement('nav');
document.createElement('article');
document.createElement('footer');
</script>
```

IE will magically apply styles to those elements, provided that there is a <body> element in the markup. You only need to create each element once, no matter how many times it appears on a page.

> **NOTE** The <script> element no longer requires you to specify the type of script; JavaScript is assumed by default. This works on legacy browsers also so you can use it right away.

Remember, HTML5 itself doesn't require a body element, but this heady brew of Internet Explorer 8 (and earlier versions), CSS, HTML5, and JavaScript does.

Although this JavaScript is unnecessary for other browsers, it won't cause them any harm. However, you might wish to give your page a speed optimisation and only download and execute this script in IE by surrounding it with conditional comments (see **http://dev.opera.com/articles/view/supporting-ie-with-conditional-comments/**).

Whenever you use a new HTML5 element, you'll need to remember to add the document.createElement for it in the <head>. Alternatively, you can use Remy's tiny HTML5-enabling script **http://remysharp.com/2009/01/07/html5-enabling-script/** that will perform this for all new elements in one fell swoop.

> ### Warning
>
> Users of all versions of Internet Explorer (currently IE8 and its antecedents) will require JavaScript to be enabled for this technique to work, although IE9 works like the other browsers and doesn't need JavaScript.

Also note that the print modules of IE seem not to be affected by our JavaScript voodoo, so pages which are styled on the screen do not carry those styles to the printer. IE Print Protector (**http://www.iecss.com/print-protector/**) is a piece of JavaScript that allows you to print HTML5 pages in IE. (This is also included in Remy's HTML5 shiv.) A user with JavaScript turned off, whether by choice or corporate security policy, will be able to access your content but will see a partially styled or unstyled page. This may or may not be a deal-breaker for you. Simon Pieters has shown that, if you know what the DOM looks like, you can style some HTML5 without JavaScript but it's not particularly scalable or maintainable; see "Styling HTML5 markup in IE without script" at **http://blog.whatwg.org/styling-ie-noscript**.

Styling HTML5 in old versions of Firefox and Camino

NOTE See Remy's HTML5doctor article "How to get HTML5 working in IE and Firefox 2" at **http:// html5doctor.com/how-to- get-html5-working-in-ie-and- firefox-2/** for more information.

Firefox and Camino both use the Gecko rendering engine, which had a bug that wouldn't render HTML5 unless it was perfect XHTML and served as XML. Firefox 3+ and Camino 2 use a more up-to-date version of Gecko that has fixed this bug, and users of those browsers upgrade frequently so this is much less of a problem than the IE weirdness.

Other legacy browser problems

There are other legacy browser problems when styling HTML5. In some circumstances, setting a background colour on elements does nothing unless you explicitly set the background-color to inherit on the children, even though that is supposedly the default behaviour. In some Gecko-based browsers, styling block-level anchors (that is, <a> elements that surround block-level elements as HTML5 now allows—see Chapter 2, "Text") can be problematic, and in all current browsers you must explicitly set such anchors to be display:block—see **http://mattwilcox.net/sandbox/html5-block-anchor/test.html**.

We don't propose to compose an exhaustive list of these behaviours; they are temporary problems that we expect quickly to disappear as new versions come out. If, as an early-adopter developer, you come across such bugs, you might wish to file a bug report; John Resig has a good article on how to do this: "A Web Developer's Responsibility"at **http://ejohn.org/blog/ a-web-developers-responsibility/**.

When to use the new HTML5 structural elements

We've used these elements to mark up our page, and styled them, and although the use of each might seem to be self-evident from the names, it's time to study them in a little more detail.

<header>

In our example above, as on most sites, the header will be the first element on a page, and contains the title of the site, logos, links back to the home page, etc. The specification says:

"The header element represents a group of introductory or navigational aids ... Note: A header element is intended to usually contain the section's heading (an h1–h6 element or an hgroup element), but this is not required. The header element can also be used to wrap a section's table of contents, a search form, or any relevant logos."

Let's dissect this. The first thing to note is that a header element is not required; in our example above, it's superfluous as it surrounds just the <h1>. Its value is that it groups "introductory or navigational" elements, so here's a more realistic example:

```
<header>
<a href="/"><img src=logo.png alt="home"></a>
<h1>My interesting blog</h1>
</header>
```

Many websites have a title and a tagline or subtitle. To mask the subtitle from the outlining algorithm (so making the main heading and subtitle into one logical unit; see Chapter 2 for more discussion), the main heading and subtitle can be grouped in the new <hgroup> element:

```
<header>
<a href="/"><img src=logo.png alt="home"></a>
<hgroup>
<h1>My interesting blog</h1>
<h2>Tedium, dullness and monotony</h2>
</hgroup>
</header>
```

The header can also contain navigation. This can be very useful for site-wide navigation, especially on template-driven sites where the whole of the <header> element could come from a template file. So, for example, the horizontal site-wide navigation on **www.thaicookery.co.uk** could be coded as in **Figure 1.6**.

```
<header>
 <hgroup>
  <h1>Thai cookery school</h1>
  <h2>Learn authentic Thai cookery in your own home</h2>
 </hgroup>
 <nav>
  <ul>
   <li>Home</li>
   <li><a href="courses.html">Cookery courses</a></li>
   <li><a href="contact.html">Contact</a></li>
  </ul>
 </nav>
</header>
```

FIGURE 1.6
www.thaicookery.co.uk's header.

Of course, it's not required that the <nav> be in the <header>. The Thai cookery example could just as easily be marked up with the main <nav> outside the <header>:

```
<header>
<hgroup>
<h1>Thai cookery school></h1>
<h2>Learn authentic Thai cookery in your own home</h2>
</hgroup>
</header>
<nav>
<ul>
<li>Home</li>
<li><a href="courses.html">Cookery courses</a></li>
```

```
<li><a href="contact.html">Contact</a></li>
</ul>
</nav>
```

It depends largely on whether you believe that site-wide navigation belongs in the site-wide header and also pragmatic considerations about ease of styling. Take, for example, my personal site, which has a very long site-wide navigation on the left of the content area, which can be much longer than a post. Putting this <nav> in the <header> would make it very hard to put the main content in the right place and have a footer, so in this case, the site-wide navigation is outside the <header>, and is a sibling child of the <body>, as in this example (**Figure 1.7**).

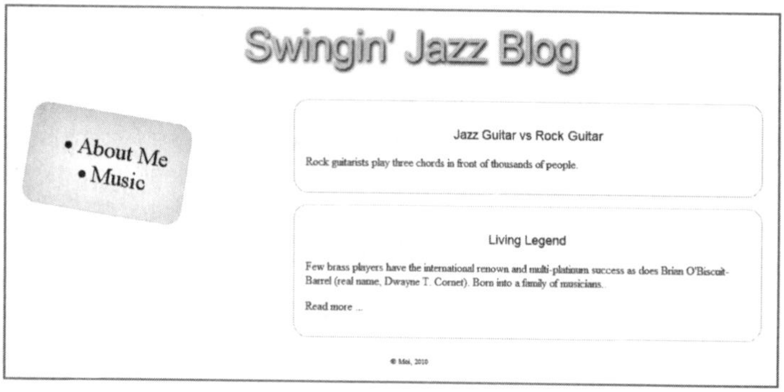

FIGURE 1.7 Typical page with site-wide navigation out of the main header area.

Note that we're currently only creating the main <header> for the page; there can be multiple <header>s—we'll come to that in Chapter 2.

<nav>

The <nav> element is designed to mark up navigation. Navigation is defined as being links around a page (so, for example, a table of contents at the top of an article that links to anchor points on the same page) or within a site. But not every collection of links is <nav>; a list of sponsored links isn't <nav>. Neither is a page of search results, as that is the main content of the page.

As with <header>s and <footer>s (and all of the new elements), you're not restricted to one <nav> per page. You might very well have site-wide <nav> in a header, a <nav> which is a table of contents for the current article, and a <nav> below that which links to other related articles on your site.

> ## To <nav> or not to <nav>?
>
> The spec suggests that the "legal" links (copyright, contact, freedom of information, privacy policies, etc.) that are often tucked away in the footer should not be wrapped in a <nav>: "It is common for footers to have a short list of links to various pages of a site, such as the terms of service, the home page, and a copyright page. The footer element alone is sufficient for such cases, without a nav element."
>
> We disagree with this suggestion. Many sites also include a link to accessibility information that gives information such as how to request information in alternate formats, and people who require such information are those who would benefit the most from user agents that can take them directly to elements marked up as <nav>.

The contents of a <nav> element will probably be a list of links, marked up as an unordered list (which has become a tradition since Mark Newhouse's seminal "Taming Lists" (**http://www.alistapart.com/articles/taminglists/**) or, in the case of breadcrumb trails, an ordered list. Note that the <nav> element is a wrapper; it doesn't replace the <ol> or <ul> element, but wraps around it. That way, legacy browsers that don't understand the element will just see the list element and list items and behave themselves just fine.

While it makes sense to use a list (and it gives you more hooks for CSS) it's not mandatory. This is perfectly valid:

```
<nav>
<p><a href="/">Home</a></p>
<p><a href="/about">About</a></p>
</nav>
```

You can include headings for navigation, too:

```
<nav>
<h2>Main navigation</h2>
<ul>
<li><a href="/about">About me</a></li>
<li><a href="/news">News</a></li>
</ul>
</nav>
```

Grouping <nav> and other elements in a sidebar

Many sites have a sidebar that includes multiple blocks of navigation and other non-navigation content. Take, for example, my personal site **www.brucelawson.co.uk** (**Figure 1.8**).

FIGURE 1.8 My blog sidebar, mixing navigation with colophon information and pictures of hunks.

The sidebar on the left of the main content has many nav areas (not pictured) such as pages, categories, archives, and most recent comments. These are marked up as a series of <nav> elements (a single <nav> containing a list with sublist is also possible but I prefer to use discrete <nav> elements for each type of nav).

The <nav> elements contained in the new <aside> element "can be used for typographical effects like pull quotes or sidebars, for advertising, for groups of nav elements, and for other content that is considered separate from the main content of the page." **http://dev.w3.org/html5/spec/semantics.html# the-aside-element**.

```
<aside>
<nav>
<h2>Pages</h2>
<ul> .. </ul>
</nav>

...
```

```
<nav>
<h2>Recent comments</h2>
<ul> ... </ul>
</nav>

<section>
<h2>blah blah</h2>
<a href="...">Web hosting by LovelyHost</a>
<img src="...">
<p>Powered by <a href="...">WordPress</a></p>
<p><a href="...">Entries (RSS)</a> and <a href="...">
¬ Comments (RSS)</a></p>
</section>
</aside>
```

Note that the "Blah blah" section is not marked up as <nav>, as the link to my web host, a picture of me, and two RSS links are not "sections that consist of major navigation blocks" as the spec defines <nav>. It's wrapped in a <section> in order that the sidebar headings remain the same level in the outlining algorithm (see Chapter 2 for more). Another way to mark up this sidebar would be to use one single over-arching <nav> rather than multiple <nav> elements. As any feline taxidermist will tell you, there is more than one way to skin a cat.

<footer>

The <footer> element is defined in the spec as representing "a footer for its nearest ancestor sectioning content or sectioning root element." ("Sectioning content" includes article, aside, nav, section, and "sectioning root elements" are blockquote, body, details, fieldset, figure, td).

Note that, as with the header element, there can be more than one footer on a page; we'll revisit that in Chapter 2. For now, we're just having one footer on the page that is a child of the body element. As the spec says, "When the nearest ancestor sectioning content or sectioning root element is the body element, then it applies to the whole page."

The spec continues "A footer typically contains information about its section such as who wrote it, links to related documents, copyright data, and the like."

Our footer holds copyright data, which we're wrapping in a <small> element, too. <small> has been redefined in HTML5;

previously it was a presentational element, but in HTML5 it represents small print: "Small print typically features disclaimers, caveats, legal restrictions, or copyrights. Small print is also sometimes used for attribution, or for satisfying licensing requirements."

Your site's footer probably has more than just a single copyright notice. You might have links to privacy policies, accessibility information (why are you hiding that out of the way?), and other such links. These should be wrapped in <nav>, despite the spec's advice (see previous <nav> section).

You might even have a fashionable "fat footer" like **www.thecssdiv.co.uk** (**Figure 1.9**).

FIGURE 1.9 The "fat footer" of thecssdiv.co.uk.

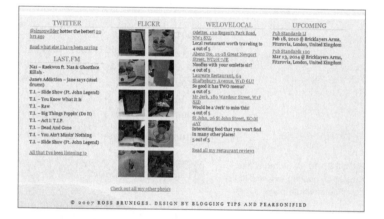

It is legitimate to wrap the links to other pages on the site with an <aside> inside the footer—but ask yourself whether the <aside> is part of the footer, or whether it would be better for the <aside> to instead be a sibling of the <footer>. After all, the links to other pages are presumably tangentially related to the whole page rather than just the content of the footer.

Here, I would use the following markup:

```
<body>
 <div id=mainContent>
  ...
 </div>
<aside>
 <nav>
  <h2>Twitter </h2>
  <ul> ... </ul>
 </nav>
```

```
<nav>
 <h2>Flickr </h2>
 <ul> ... </ul>
</nav>
<nav>
 <h2>WeLoveLocal</h2>
 <ul> ... </ul>
</nav>
<nav>
 <h2>Upcoming </h2>
 <ul> ... </ul>
</nav>
</aside>

<footer>
 <small>&copy;2007 Ross Bruniges. Design by Blogging Tips
and Pearsonified</small>
</footer>

</body>
```

Figure 1.10 shows how to avoid a "fat footer."

FIGURE 1.10 Avoiding a "fat footer" by making external links an aside of whole page

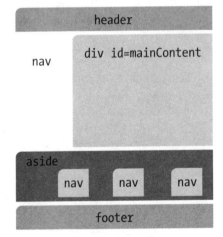

<article>

The main content of this blog's home page contains a few blog posts. We wrap each one up in an <article> element. <article> is specified thus: "The article element represents a component of a page that consists of a self-contained composition in a document, page, application, or site and that is intended to be independently distributable or reusable, e.g., in syndication."

A blog post, a tutorial, a news story, comic strip, or a video with its transcript all fit perfectly into this definition. Less intuitively, so can individual emails in a Web-based email client, maps and re-usable Web widgets. For <article> don't think newspaper article, think article of clothing—a discrete item. Note that, as with <nav>, the heading goes inside the element, so

```
<h1>My article</h1>
<article>
 <p>Blah blah</p>
</article>
```

is incorrect; it should be

```
<article>
 <h1>My article</h1>
 <p>Blah blah</p>
</article>
```

There are many more interesting facets to <article> which (you've guessed it) we'll look at in the next chapter.

Summary

In this chapter, we've taken our first look at HTML5, and its DOCTYPE. We've seen its forgiving syntax rules such as optional uppercase/lowercase, quoting and attribute mini-misation, omitting implied elements like head/body, omitting standard stuff like type="text/javascript" and "text/css" on the <script>, and <style> tags. We've structured the main land-marks of a web page using <header>, <footer>, <nav>, <aside>, and <article>, providing user agents with more semantics than the meaningless generic <div> element that was our only option in HTML 4 and styled the new elements with the magic of CSS. Not bad for one chapter, eh?

CHAPTER 2

Text

Bruce Lawson

NOW THAT YOU'VE marked up the main page landmarks with HTML5 and seen how a document's outline can be structured, this lesson looks deeper to show how you can further structure your main content.

To do this, you'll mark up a typical blog with HTML5. We've chosen a blog because over 70 percent of web professionals have a blog (**www.aneventapart.com/alasurvey2008**), and everyone has seen one. It's also a good archetype of modern websites with headers, footers, sidebars, multiple navigation areas, and a form, whether it's a blog, a news site, or a brochure site (with products instead of news pieces).

Structuring main content areas

Take a look at the main content area of a blog (**Figure 2.1**). There may be multiple articles, each containing "metadata" and the actual textual content of that article.

FIGURE 2.1 A series of articles on a typical blog.

FIGURE 2.1 A series of articles on a typical blog.

Here's some typical markup (simplified from the default Word-Press theme)

```
<div class="post">
<h2>Memoirs of a Parisian lion-tamer</h2>
<small>January 24th, 2010</small>
  <div class="entry">
    <p>Claude Bottom's poignant autobiography is this
    ¬ summer's must-read.</p>
  </div>
  <p class="postmetadata">Posted in <a href="/?cat=3">
  ¬ Books category</a> | <a    href="/?p=34#respond">
  ¬ No Comments</a></p>
</div>
```

There is nothing major wrong with this markup (although we query use in HTML 4 of the presentational <small> element for the date). It will work fine in "HTML5" browsers, but apart from the heading for the blog post, there is no real structure—just meaningless <div>s and paragraphs. HTML 4 gives us generic structures to mark up content. <div>, for example, is just a generic "box" that tells the browser "here's some stuff, it all belongs together," but it doesn't mean anything; there's no semantic value beyond "these belong together." Where possible, we'll replace generic boxes with new HTML5 elements, while still using <div> where there isn't an appropriate element, just as we did in HTML 4.

Let's concentrate on an individual article first. As you saw in Chapter 1, you can replace the outer <div class="post"> with <article>, but you can still go further. The HTML5 <header> and <footer> elements can be used multiple times on a page, each time referring to the section it's in.

The heading and the time of posting is "introductory matter" and thus the job for <header>, right? Similarly, the metadata about the post that is currently in a paragraph with class"=postmetadata" is better marked up in HTML5 as a <footer>, which "typically contains information about its section, such as who wrote it, links to related documents, copyright data, and the like."

Diagrammatically, the revised structure is shown in **Figure 2.2**.

FIGURE 2.2 A single blog article using new HTML5 structures.

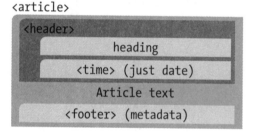

```
<article>
  <header>
    <h2>Memoirs of a Parisian lion-tamer</h2>
    <time datetime=2010-01-24>January 24th,
    ¬ 2010</time>
  </header>
  <p>Claude Bottom's poignant autobiography is this
  ¬ summer's must-read.</p>
  <footer>
    Posted in <a href="/?cat=3" >Books category</a>.
    ¬ <a href="/?p=34#respond">No  Comments</a>
  </footer>
</article>
```

Let's look at this in more detail.

The <time> element

<time> is a new element for unambiguously encoding dates and times for machines, while still displaying them in a human-readable way. The uses of this in web pages aren't hard to imagine: a browser could offer to add future events to a user's calendar; content aggregators could produce visual timelines of events; a Thai-localised browser could offer to transform dates into Thai Buddhist era dates, which are numerically 543 years greater than their corresponding Western-style years.

The spec says "The time element represents either a time on a 24-hour clock, or a precise date in the proleptic Gregorian calendar, optionally with a time and a time-zone offset."

The machine-readable part of the <time> element is usually encapsulated in the element's datetime attribute. The content inside the element is what gets presented to end users.

```
<time datetime=2009-11-13>13 November 2009</time>
<time datetime=2009-11-13>13<sup>th</sup> November last
¬ year</time>
<time datetime=2010-11-13>Bruce's 21st birthday</time>
<time datetime=2010-11-13T020:00Z>8PM on my birthday</time>
<time datetime=20:00>8 PM</time>
```

If you're happy to have the machine-readable format visible to the end user as well, you don't need to use a separate datetime attribute. User agents should then simply pick the content of the element and interpret it:

```
<time>20:00</time>
```

Machine-readable dates and times

To be machine-readable, dates must be in the format YYYY-MM-DD and may also include a time, prefixed with "T" to separate the date and time, in the format HH:MM. Optionally you can append seconds (separated from the minutes with a colon). Fractions of a second are allowed after a full stop mark.

As you've seen above, you can give a time on the 24-hour clock with no date information.

If you're giving time and date together, you need to show the time zone: that's either "Z" for Coordinated Universal Time (UTC), or an offset from UTC in hours and minutes, prefixed with a plus or minus.

Putting that all together: "1979-10-14T12:00:00.001-04:00" represents one millisecond after noon on October 14th, 1979, in Eastern Standard Time during daylight saving time (UTC—4 hours).

The only trouble with `<time>` is that it must contain a positive date on the Proleptic Gregorian calendar—meaning you can't encode a date before the Christian Era. Neither can you encode imprecise dates such as "July 1904." This seriously limits its use for sites such as museums, history/encyclopedia pages, or family trees, where precise dates may not be known.

The pubdate attribute

pubdate is a Boolean attribute to indicate that this particular `<time>` is the publication date of an `<article>` or the whole `<body>` content.

You might be wondering why the pubdate attribute is needed at all. Why not just assume that any `<time>` element in an `<article>`'s `<header>` is its publication date?

Consider this example:

```
<article>
   <header>
     <h1>Come to my party on <time datetime=2010-12-01>1
     ¬ December</time></h1>
      <p>Published on <time datetime=2010-06-20 pubdate>20
      ¬ June 2010</time></p>
   </header>
   <p>I'm throwing a party at Dr Einstein's Cabaret
   ¬ Roller-disco Bierkeller Pizza-parlour-a-gogo. Do come
   ¬ and dance to Rusty Trombone's Swingin' Brass Band.
   ¬ (Formal dress and lewd hat required.)</p>
</article>
```

You'll see that there are two dates within the `<header>`: the date of the actual party and the publication date of the article. The pubdate attribute is required to remove any ambiguity. And yes, you are invited—just don't get drunk this time.

More fun with headers and footers

This main surprise with our article makeover is that each article can have its own `<header>` and `<footer>`. This means that, in addition to the "main" header and footer on a page, each article can have its own headers and footers. They can be separately styled with CSS: body>header and body>footer target the "main" headers and footers (assuming that they're direct descendants of `<body>`), whereas article>header and article>footer target the inner structures.

To include old versions of IE, you can take advantage of specificity. Define generic header and footer styles, and then redefine/override them for article header and article footer:

```
header {display:block; color:red; text-align:right;}
¬/*page header */
article header {color:blue; text-align:center;}
¬/*article header */
```

Note that so far, you've introduced no ids or classes as hooks for CSS.

Using multiple <footer>s on the same element

The spec says "Footers don't necessarily have to appear at the end of a section, though they usually do," and it allows an element to have two or more footers. A simplified version of the example in the spec is

```
<body>
 <footer><a href="/">Back to index...</a></footer>
 <h1>Lorem ipsum</h1>
 <p>Lorem ipsum</p>
 <footer><a href="/">Back to index...</a></footer>
</body>
```

The reason for this is that the elements are supposed to be non-presentational. If "back to index" is the footer below the article, and you choose to have "back to index" above the article, too, you should use the same element for the same content, regardless of where it appears.

Using <blockquote> <footer>s

Very groovily, <blockquote> can have a footer, which is a very useful way of citing the source in a way that's unambiguously associated with the quotation but also nicely presented to your users (previously, the cite attribute on <blockquote> wasn't displayed anywhere):

```
<blockquote>
  Thou look'st like antichrist, in that lewd hat.
  <footer>Ananias <cite>Scene 4.3, <a  href="http://
  ¬www.gutenberg.org/files/4081/4081-h/4081-h.htm">The
  ¬Alchemist</a></cite> (Ben Jonson)</footer>
</blockquote>
```

Adding blogposts and comments

So, you have a page with a header, footer, navigation, content area containing several articles (blog posts), each with its own header and footer. But wait...what is a blog without comments?

The specification mentions this case, and recommends the use of nested <article>s: "When article elements are nested, the inner article elements represent articles that are in principle related to the contents of the outer article. For instance, a blog entry on a site that accepts user-submitted comments could represent the comments as article elements nested within the article element for the blog entry."

So let's do that. Note as well that blog comments are typically shown in chronological order and have information such as author's name and URL—in short, header information. Diagrammatically it looks like what is shown in **Figure 2.3**.

FIGURE 2.3 The structure of a blog post, with comments as nested articles.

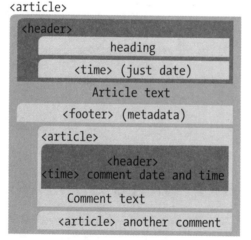

The code is as you'd expect, with comments highlighted:

```
<article>
  <header>
    <h1>Come to my party on <time datetime=
    ¬2010-12-01>1 December</time></h1>
    <p>Published on <time datetime=2010-06-20 pubdate>
    ¬20 June 2010</time></p>
  </header>
```

```
<p>I'm throwing a party at Dr Einstein's Cabaret
¬Roller-disco Bierkeller Pizza-parlour-a-gogo. Do come
¬and dance to Rusty Trombone's Swingin' Brass Band.
¬(Formal dress and lewd hat required.)</p>
<footer>Published in the Parrtay!! category by Bruce
¬</footer>

<article> <!-- comment -->
 <header>
  Comment from <a href="http://remysharp.com">Remy
  ¬Sharp</a> at <time datetime="2010-05-01T08:45Z">
  ¬8.45 on 1 May 2010</time>
 </header>
 <p>I'll be there. I very much enjoy a bit of Rusty
 ¬Trombone.</p>
</article> <!-- end comment -->

<article> <!-- comment -->
 <header>
  Comment from <a href="http://splintered.co.uk">Patrick
  ¬Lauke</a> at <time datetime="2010-05-02T10:45Z">10.45
  ¬on 2 May 2010</time>
 </header>
 <p>Sorry mate. Am washing my hair.</p>
</article> <!-- end comment -->

</article> <!-- end blogpost -->
```

Working with HTML5 outlines

Some word processing applications have a function to show you the outline of a document. For example, **Figure 2.4** shows this chapter in Microsoft Word 2007's outline view.

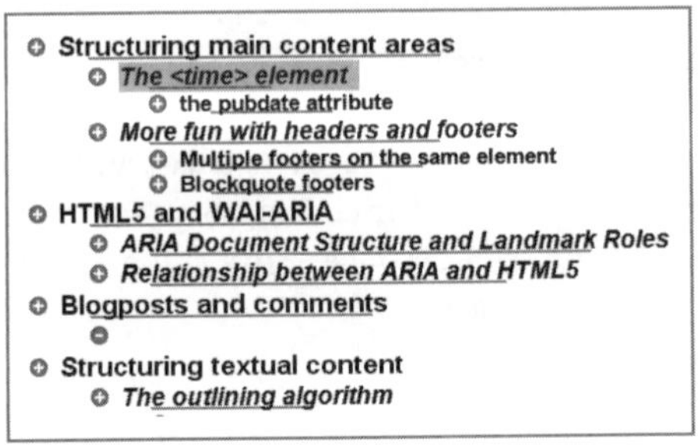

FIGURE 2.4 Microsoft Word 2007's outline view.

HTML5 has a tightly-defined outlining algorithm that allows user agents to produce a similar outline from a web page. Just as with a word-processing package, this could be used to give the user a quick overview of the web page (and, of course, there's no reason why the web page shouldn't actually be a word-processing application). The other main use for the outlining algorithm is for syndication: grabbing content and inserting it somewhere else and ensuring that the destination web page still has a logical structure.

This section of the chapter is pretty dense, and it hasn't been implemented by any browsers yet (although there is a JavaScript implementation at **http://code.google.com/p/h5o/**). You need to understand the concept of the document outline in order to know when to use ‹section›, ‹aside›, or ‹div›.

One major departure from HTML4, and an important concept to grasp before you proceed, is that certain HTML5 elements— ‹article›, ‹section›, ‹nav›, and ‹aside›—are *sectioning content*, which begin new sections in the outline. To explain this concept, let's take this simple code:

```
<h1>Hello</h1>
<div>
  <h1>World</h1>
</div>
```

1. Hello
2. World

FIGURE 2.5 A simple outline.

To illustrate how this algorithm works, I'm using a web-based utility at **gsnedders.html5.org/outliner/**, as no browsers currently have this logic embedded. The outline this code generates is as you would expect (**Figure 2.5**).

Figure 2.6 shows what happens if you change the meaningless ‹div› to an ‹article›, which is sectioning content:

1. Hello
   1. World

FIGURE 2.6 A document outline after ‹div› is replaced by ‹article›.

```
<h1>Hello</h1>
<article>
  <h1>World</h1>
</article>
```

You can see that the presence of sectioning content has shifted its content to be hierarchically "below" the content that preceded it. Or, to put it more simply: the ‹h1› inside the article is a logical ‹h2› because ‹article› has started a new section. Using ‹section›, ‹nav›, or ‹aside› instead of ‹article› does the same thing, as they are all sectioning content.

In fact, it doesn't matter what level of heading you use here; the outlining algorithm cares about nesting and relative levels, so this code

```
<h3>Hello</h3>
<article>
 <h6>World</h6>
</article>
```

produces exactly the same result as Figure 2.6.

You might be saying, "So what. What's the use for that?" Well, firstly, it means you're not restricted to six levels of headings, as you are in HTML 4. A heading element nested inside seven levels of <section>, <article>, <nav>, or <aside> (or any combination of them) becomes a logical <h7> element (however, unless you're marking up legal documents or some other horrors, you should reconsider your content if you need so many levels).

Another advantage is with syndication. Suppose Remy posts an article:

```
<article>
 <h1>What I did on my holiday</h1>
 <p>I went to Narnia. I was bitten by a trilobite. Then I
 ¬ came home.</p>
</article>
```

Let's say you run a large online newspaper and naturally wish to syndicate this story. When the magic syndication machines slot it into your template, the resulting code is

```
<h1>The Monotonous Times</h1>
<section>
 <h2>Breaking news</h2>
  <article>
   <h1>What I did on my holiday</h1>
   <p>I went to Narnia. I was bitten by a trilobite.
   ¬ Then I came home.</p>
  </article>
 ..
</section>
```

It's obvious that "breaking news" is higher in the hierarchy of headings than the title of Remy's blog post, but due to a mismatch between Remy's template and your template, there's an <h2> that is more important than the <h1>.

Checking the outline, however, shows us that everything is as it should be (**Figure 2.7**). You clever thing, you.

FIGURE 2.7 The outlining algorithm produces the correct outline in syndication, too.

```
1. The Monotonous Times
   1. Breaking news
      1. What I did on my holiday
```

<nav>, <aside> and untitled sections

A quick word about the outlining tool at **gsnedders.html5.org/outliner/**, as you'll probably get into the habit of checking your document's outline as part of your development process, much as you regularly validate your code and check it in different browsers.

If it finds sectioning content that has no heading, it will report it:

```
<article>
  <p>I have no heading</p>
</article>
```

This gives the outline "Untitled Section." For <section>s and <article>s, this is a useful warning as these elements nearly always begin with a heading.

However, inside <nav> and <aside> it's perfectly legitimate not to have a heading. You may want to do it for some <nav> blocks, such as "Most popular posts" or "Recent comments," but you probably don't want a redundant heading on your main site <nav> that just says "Navigation."

Therefore, if you see "Untitled Section," don't automatically assume that you should put a heading there. Treat it as a warning, not an error. A bug has been filed to give a friendlier message for untitled sections in <nav>, but so far has not been addressed.

<hgroup>

Sometimes you have a heading and a subheading, or tag line. Slashdot uses "News for nerds. Stuff that matters"; dev.Opera has "Follow the Standards. Break the Rules"; Metafilter is a "community weblog." How do you mark up those taglines? In HTML 4, you could use

```
<h1>Metafilter</h1>
<p>community weblog</p>
```

but that doesn't feel right, as the subtitle feels like it should be a heading. An alternate method of marking this up could be

```
<h1>Metafilter</h1>
<h2>community weblog</h2>
```

but then every header on the site would need to be `<h3>` to `<h6>` as they're subordinate to the tagline. In HTML5, the subtitle can be marked up as a heading element but removed from the document outline, like so:

```
<hgroup>
 <h1>Metafilter</h1>
 <h2>community weblog</h2>
</hgroup>
```

This gives the outline shown in **Figure 2.8**.

The spec for `<hgroup>` says "For the purposes of document summaries, outlines, and the like, the text of hgroup elements is defined to be the text of the highest-ranked h1–h6 element descendant of the hgroup element."

So:

```
<article>
 <hgroup>
  <h2>Get the beers in! Here comes</h2>
  <h1>Remy Sharp!</h1>
 </hgroup>
</article>
```

shows the text "Remy Sharp" in the outline, as that's the highest-ranking heading element in the group.

1. Metafilter

FIGURE 2.8 The outline shows only "Metafilter" as part of the outline.

> **NOTE** We haven't used a `<header>` element in this `<article>`. `<header>` is a grouping element that collects together introductory content; as you only have headings, already grouped in `<hgroup>`, there is no need for a further layer of grouping. It wouldn't be an error to use it, but it's superfluous in this example.

Sectioning roots

Note that certain elements—`<blockquote>`, `<body>`, `<details>`, `<fieldset>`, `<figure>`, `<td>`—are said to be *sectioning roots*, and can have their own outlines, but the sections and headings inside these elements do not contribute to the outlines of their ancestors. This is because, for example, you could quote several sections of an article in a `<blockquote>`, but those quoted sections don't form part of the overall document outline.

In the following example:

```
<h1>Unicorns and butterflies</h1>
<nav>
 <h2>Main nav</h2>
 ...
</nav>
<article>
 <h2>Fairies love rainbows!</h2>
 <p>According to Mr Snuggles the fluffy kitten, fairies
 ¬like:</p>
 <blockquote>
  <h3>Pretty dainty things</h3>
  <p>Fairies love rainbows, ribbons, and ballet shoes</p>
  <h3>Weaponry</h3>
  <p>Fairies favour Kalashnikovs, flick knives, and
  ¬depleted uranium missiles</p>
 </blockquote>
</article>
```

the outline does not include the contents of blockquote:
(**Figure 2.9**).

FIGURE 2.9 The outline does not include content in a sectioning root.

```
1. Unicorns and butterflies
  1. Main nav
  2. Fairies love rainbows!
```

Styling headings in HTML5

All this clever stuff presents a challenge to authors of CSS. Given that

```
<article><section><h1>...</h1></section></article>
<article><article><h1>...</h1></article></article>
<section><section><h1>...</h1></section></section>
<section><aside><h1>...</h1></aside></section>
<h3>...</h3>
```

can potentially be the same logical levels, you might naturally wish to apply the same styling (you may equally wish not to). This can lead to gigantic blocks of rules in your style sheets. There has been some talk of a new CSS pseudo-class or pseudo-element like :heading(n), which would be possible (because the browser "knows" what level a heading is from the outlining algorithm) and which would simplify styling:

```
*:heading(1) {font-size: 2.5em;}   /* a logical <h1> */
*:heading(2) {font-size: 2em;}     /* a logical <h2> */
```

However, at time of writing, this is but a wonderful dream. As a stop-gap, Mozilla is experimenting with a new selector grouping mechanism to Firefox nightlies called `:-moz-any()` that allows a form of CSS shorthand—see **hacks.mozilla.org/2010/05/moz-any-selector-grouping/**.

Perhaps, for this reason, you would be tempted to use only <h1> elements to simplify styling, and let the outlining algorithm do the rest. After all, the spec says "Sections may contain headings of any rank, but authors are strongly encouraged to either use only h1 elements, or to use elements of the appropriate rank for the section's nesting level." But you shouldn't (yet) as it harms accessibility.

The outlining algorithm and accessibility

> **NOTE** Watch the excellent video entitled "Importance of HTML Headings for Accessibility," available at **www.youtube. com/watch?v=AmUPhEVWu_E**. The video shows how a blind accessibility consultant navigates a page with JAWS. In an ideal world, it would be compulsory to watch and understand this video before you're allowed to call yourself a professional designer or developer. Sadly, it's not an ideal world.

A recent survey by WebAim showed that 76 percent of screen reader users "always or often" navigate by headings (see the full survey for more vital information at **www.webaim.org/projects/ screenreadersurvey2/**). These people use the hierarchy of headings both to give themselves a mental overview (an outline!) of the document they're in and also to navigate through that content. Most screen readers have keyboard shortcuts that allow users to jump from heading to heading. For example, the JAWS screen reader uses the H key to jump from heading to heading, the 1 key to jump to the next <h1>, the 2 key to go to the next <h2>, and so on.

Currently, no browser builds an internal model of the page structure based on all the complex rules previously mentioned and therefore can't expose this model to any screen reader or assistive technology. So, using only <h1> wrecks the navigability and therefore hinders the accessibility of your page.

Our advice is again, follow the spec: "Use elements of the appropriate rank for the section's nesting level." That is, ensure that, in your pages, the hierarchy of headings is correct even without factoring in new HTML5 elements. It will also make writing CSS much easier.

In cases when articles are syndicated from one site to the other and the levels might be out of logical order, a completely unscientific Twitter poll of screen reader users suggested that badly nested section headers is better than all headings being at the same level (which is still better than no headings at all).

And, having done your best, wait for the browsers and the screen readers that sit on top of them to implement the outlining algorithm. As I said, it's not an ideal world.

What's the difference between <article> and <section>?

This is a question that is regularly asked of us at **html5doctor.com**.

An article is an independent, stand-alone piece of discrete content. Think of a blog post, or a news item in a document-based site. In a web application, an <article> could be individual emails within an email application or stories in a web-based feed reader, as each email or story is both a component of the application and can be independently reused.

<article>

Consider this real-world blog/news article:

```
<article>
<h1>Bruce Lawson is World's Sexiest Man</h1>
<p>Legions of lovely ladies voted luscious lothario Lawson
¬as the World's Sexiest Man today.</p>
<h2>Second-sexiest man concedes defeat</h2>
<p>Remington Sharp, jQuery glamourpuss and Brighton
¬roister-doister, was gracious in defeat. "It's cool being
¬the second sexiest man when number one is Awesome Lawson"
¬he said from his swimming pool-sized jacuzzi full of
¬supermodels.</p>
</article>
```

It could be syndicated, either by RSS or other means, and makes sense without further contextualisation. Just as you can syndicate partial feeds, a "teaser" article is still an article:

```
<article>
<a href=full-story.html>
 <h1>Bruce Lawson is World's Sexiest Man</h1>
 <p><img src=bruce.png alt="bruce lawson">Legions of lovely
 ¬ladies voted luscious lothario Lawson as the World's
 ¬Sexiest  Man today.</p>
```

```
<p>Read more</p>
</a>
</article>
```

"Block-level" links

Note from this example that you can wrap links round "block-level" elements. In the HTML 4 spec, this is not allowed, so you would probably have links around the heading, the teaser paragraph, and the phrase "read more" all pointing to the same destination.

In HTML5 the single link can surround the whole `<article>`. As the browsers already handle wrapping links around block-level elements, and there is an obvious use-case, there was no reason to artificially keep the structure as invalid.

XHTML 2 had a comparable mechanism, which allowed `href` on any element but, of course, this isn't backward-compatible; current browsers simply laugh at `<div href="full-story.html">` and then ignore it. What's interesting about "block-level links" is that they work in browsers now with a hint or two—remember **http://mattwilcox.net/sandbox/html5-block-anchor/test.html**.

Well, almost. There's currently a parsing bug in Firefox that Remy calls the "Vomit Bug" (**remysharp. com/2009/08/10/defining-the-vomit-bug/**). It prevents Firefox from rendering anchors that contain some new HTML5 elements such as `<section>`. However, it's pretty weird to want to put whole sections inside link text. If you stick to HTML 4 elements such as paragraphs, headings, images, and so on, Firefox works just fine. It's also a known bug that disappears if the HTML5 parser is turned on.

As you've seen, comments on blog posts are `<article>`s inside a parent `<article>`. There are other uses for this nesting beside comments, for example a transcript to a video:

```
<article>
<h1>Stars celebrate Bruce Lawson</h1>
<video>...</video>

<article class=transcript>
<h1>Transcript</h1>
 <p>Supermodel #1: "He's so hunky!"</p>
 <p>Supermodel #2: "He's a snogtabulous bundle of gorgeous
 ¬manhood! And I saw him first, so hands off!"</p>
</article>

</article>
```

The transcript is complete in itself, even though it's related to the video in the outer `<article>`. The spec says "When article elements are nested, the inner article elements represent articles that are in principle related to the contents of the outer article."

> **NOTE** A `<section>`
> generally begins with a
> heading that introduces it. An
> exception to this might be a
> `<section>` that will have a
> heading injected using JavaS-
> cript. If you wouldn't use a head-
> ing, or you want some wrapping
> element purely for styling pur-
> poses you probably should be
> using a `<div>`.

`<section>`

`<section>`, on the other hand, isn't "a self-contained composition in a document, page, application, or site and that is intended to be independently distributable or reusable." It's either a way of sectioning a page into different subject areas, or sectioning an article into, well, sections.

Consider this HTML 4 markup—the rules from Remy's previous job in an off-Broadway production of Wizard of Oz:

```
<h1>Rules for Munchkins</h1>
<h2>Yellow Brick Road</h2>
<p>It is vital that Dorothy follows it—so no selling bricks
¬ as "souvenirs"</p>


<h2>Fan Club uniforms</h2>
<p>All Munchkins are obliged to wear their "I'm a friend of
¬ Dorothy!" t-shirt when representing the club</p>
<p><strong>Vital caveat about the information above:
¬ does not apply on the first Thursday of the month.
¬ </strong></p>
```

Does the "Vital caveat about the information above" refer to the whole article, that is, everything under the introductory `<h1>`, or does it refer only to the information under the preceding `<h2>` ("Fan Club uniforms")? In HTML 4, that paragraph would fall under the `<h2>`, and there's no easy way to semantically change this. In HTML5, the `<section>` element makes its meaning unambiguous (which is what we really mean as web developers when we use the word "semantic"):

```
<article>
<h1>Rules for Munchkins</h1>

 <section>
  <h2>Yellow Brick Road</h2>
  <p>It is vital that Dorothy follows it—so no selling
  ¬ bricks as "souvenirs"</p>
 </section>



 <section>
  <h2>Fan Club uniforms</h2>
```

```
<p>All Munchkins are obliged to wear their "I'm a friend
¬of Dorothy!" t-shirt when representing the club</p>
</section>

<p><strong>Vital caveat about the information above:
¬does not apply on the first Thursday of the month.
¬</strong></p>
</article>
```

Figure 2.10 illustrates this diagrammatically.

FIGURE 2.10 Now you can see that the vital caveat refers to the whole `<article>`.

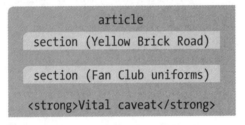

If it had been inside the final section element:

```
<article>
...
<section>
  <h2>Fan Club uniforms</h2>
  <p>All Munchkins are obliged to wear their "I'm a friend
  ¬of Dorothy!" t-shirt when representing the club</p>
  <p><strong>Vital caveat about the information above:
  ¬does not apply on the first Thursday of the month
  ¬</strong></p>
 </section>
</article>
```

it would unambiguously refer to that section alone, as illustrated in **Figure 2.11**.

FIGURE 2.11 The `<section>` element removes any ambiguity.

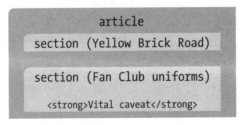

It would *not* have been correct to divide up this article with nested article elements, as they are not independent discrete entities.

OK. So you've seen that you can have <article> inside <article> and <section> inside <article>. But you can also have <article> inside <section>. What's that all about then?

<article> inside <section>

Imagine that your content area is divided into two units, one for articles about llamas, the other for articles about root vegetables. That's my kind of content.

You're not obliged to mark up your llama articles separately from your root vegetable articles, but you want to demonstrate that the two groups are thematically distinct. Perhaps, because they're thematically distinct, you want them in separate columns, or you'll use CSS and JavaScript to make a tabbed interface.

In HTML 4, you'd use our good but meaningless friend <div>. In HTML5, you use <section>, which, like <article>, invokes the HTML5 outlining algorithm (whereas <div> doesn't, because it has no special structural meaning).

```
<section>
<h1>Articles about llamas</h1>

<article>
<h2>The daily llama: buddhism and South American camelids
¬</h2>
<p>blah blah</p>
</article>

<article>
<h2>Shh! Do not alarm a llama</h2>
<p>blah blah</p>
</article>

</section>

<section>
<h1>Articles about root vegetables</h1>

<article>
<h2>Carrots: the orange miracle</h2>
```

```
<p>blah blah</p>
</article>

<article>
<h2>Eat more Swedes (the vegetables, not the people)</h2>
<p>blah blah</p>
</article>

</section>
```

Why didn't you mark the two <section>s up as <article>s instead? Because, in this example, each <section> is a collection of independent entities, each of which could be syndicated—but you wouldn't ordinarily syndicate the collection as an individual entity.

Note that a <section> doesn't need to contain lots of <article>s; it could be a collection of paragraphs explaining your creative commons licensing, an author bio, or a copyright notice. In our example, each article could contain sub-articles or sections, as explained earlier—or both.

Estelle Weyl has a nice analogy at **www.standardista.com/ html5-section-v-article**: "Think of a newspaper. The paper comes in sections. You have the sports section, real estate section, maybe home & garden section, etc. Each of those sections, in turn, has articles in it. And, some of those articles are divided into sections themselves.

In other words, you can have parent <section>s with nested <article>s that in turn have one or many <section>s. Not all pages documents need these, but it is perfectly acceptable and correct to nest this way."

Case study: www.guardian.co.uk

Let's continue with the newspaper theme and look at a real site and work out where you would use the new structures. **Figure 2.12** shows a screenshot from my favourite newspaper, "The Guardian" at **www.guardian.co.uk**. Let's see how this could be represented in HTML5.

Note that the following is how I would mark up this page; you might choose different structures, and that's OK. There's not necessarily "one true way" of doing this; it depends in part on how you intend to use the content—will you syndicate it, or pull it out of a database for display in several different page templates with a variety of heading hierarchies?

FIGURE 2.12 The Guardian homepage.

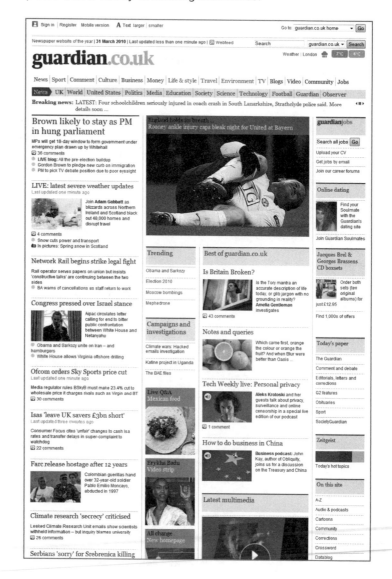

It's pretty easy to see the branding and introductory matter that forms the <header>, which also includes two <nav> structures for site-wide navigation (**Figure 2.13**).

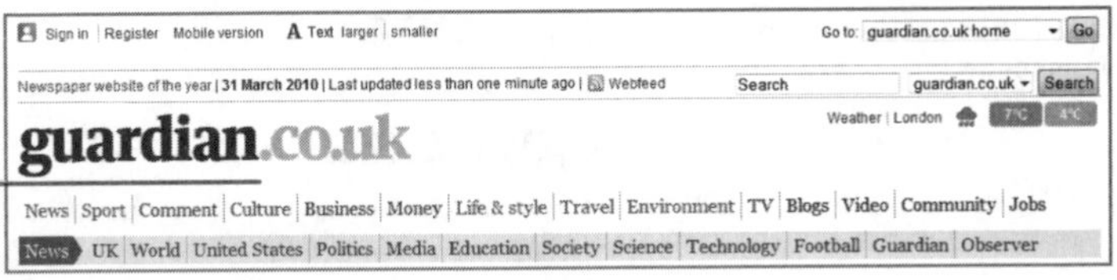

Immediately below the header is an area with the title "breaking news" and a "ticker" of text. Each summary is a link to an expanded story (**Figure 2.14**).

BREAKING NEWS

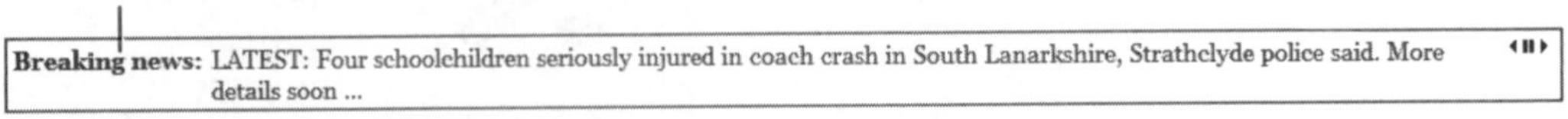

Breaking news: LATEST: Four schoolchildren seriously injured in coach crash in South Lanarkshire, Strathclyde police said. More details soon ...

FIGURE 2.14 **The "breaking news" area of Guardian homepage.**

Aside from the JavaScript-controlled ticker effect, this "breaking news" is simply a list of links to other pages. Therefore, it matches the <nav> element. Don't be fooled by the fact that it's horizontal, with the heading on the same line; CSS will sort that out:

```
<nav>
<h2>Breaking news</h2>
<ul>
 <li><a href=#>Four schoolchildren injured...</a></li>
 <li><a href=#>Terrible thing happens to someone</a></li>
 ...
</ul>
</nav>
```

Although visually this area appears closely tied with the header, it's not introductory matter or site-wide navigation. The difference is subtle, but in my opinion, links to comments, TV, and sports pages are part of site-wide navigation, while navigating news stories on a news site is "shortcut navigation" to deeper content. Therefore, this is a <nav> after rather than inside the <header> element.

There's more navigation on the right of the main content area (**Figure 2.15**).

As you saw in Chapter 1, this sidebar can be conceived of as a group of separate <nav> elements, each with its own heading (Jobs, Dating, CD box sets, Today's paper, and so on), styled with blue-grey background and thick red border-top.

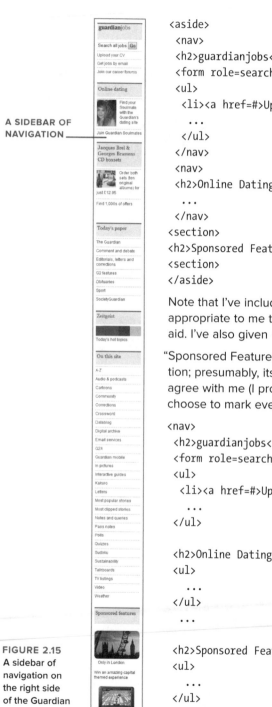

A SIDEBAR OF
NAVIGATION

FIGURE 2.15
A sidebar of
navigation on
the right side
of the Guardian
homepage.

```
<aside>
 <nav>
 <h2>guardianjobs</h2>
 <form role=search ... > ... </form>
 <ul>
  <li><a href=#>Upload your CV</a></li>
   ...
  </ul>
 </nav>
 <nav>
 <h2>Online Dating</h2>
  ...
 </nav>
<section>
<h2>Sponsored Features</h2>
<section>
</aside>
```

Note that I've included a search form in the <nav>; it seems
appropriate to me to regard a search form than a navigational
aid. I've also given it the ARIA role appropriate to its function.

"Sponsored Features" isn't inside <nav> as it's not primary navigation; presumably, its main purpose is to advertise. You may dis-
agree with me (I promise I won't get all huffy), and so you might
choose to mark everything up in one wrapping <nav>:

```
<nav>
 <h2>guardianjobs</h2>
 <form role=search ... > ... </form>
 <ul>
  <li><a href=#>Upload your CV</a></li>
   ...
 </ul>

 <h2>Online Dating</h2>
 <ul>
   ...
 </ul>
   ...

 <h2>Sponsored Features</h2>
 <ul>
   ...
 </ul>
</nav>
```

Now let's look at the main content area (**Figure 2.16**).

FIGURE 2.16 The main content area of the Guardian homepage.

MAIN CONTENT AREA

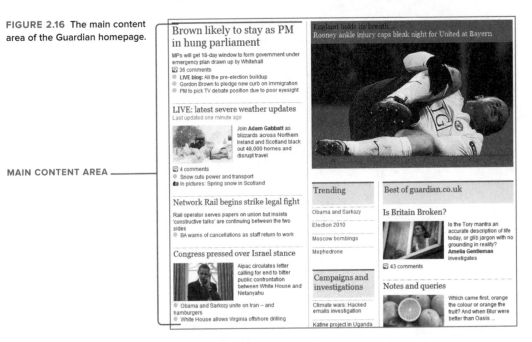

Unsurprisingly for a newspaper site, the main content area of the Guardian homepage is given over to news articles. It's important to notice that there is no overriding heading grouping the main articles (such as "top stories"), otherwise you could wrap the whole thing up in a <section>. Therefore, you just have a list of <article>s. Because <section> isn't appropriate here, if there is a need to wrap all the articles with an element for styling purposes, you'd use the semantically empty <div> element.

There is one featured article that is mostly comprised of an image, presumably because it's the most striking image available (**Figure 2.17**).

FIGURE 2.17 The featured picture.

This remains simply an <article>, although we'd probably need a class or id to allow special styling.

Below the featured article, you have some sections that aren't the top stories (there is less information on the homepage, and they're primarily, but not solely, links to other pages). They each have their own heading ("Best of guardian.co.uk," "Latest multimedia," "What you're saying"), and then a group of articles. The natural elements are therefore <article>s within <section>s:

```
<section>
<h2>Best of guardian.co.uk</h2>
<article>
<h3>Is Britain broken?</h3>
...
</article>

<article>
<h3>Notes and queries</h3>
...
</article>

<article>
<h3>Tech Weekly live: Personal privacy</h3>
...
</article>
...
</section>

<section>
<h2>Latest multimedia</h2>
...
</section>
```

On the website (but not in the screenshot), there are also a couple more <nav> blocks ("Trending," "Campaigns and Investigations") and a "fat footer" that, as we saw in Chapter 1, should be a couple of page-wide <nav> blocks outside the "real" <footer> that contains the usual privacy, terms and conditions, and accessibility information.

And there, ladies and gentlemen: an HTML5 version of **www.guardian.co.uk**. Like any other exercise in markup above the level of the trivial, there are legitimate differences of opinion. That's OK. HTML is a general language, so there aren't elements for every specific occasion.

Understanding WAI-ARIA

The W3C Web Accessibility Initiative's Accessible Rich Internet Applications suite (WAI-ARIA) is an independent spec that "plugs the holes" in HTML 4 (or any other markup language) to help web applications and web pages to be made more accessible.

Imagine that you have scripted a slider control. In HTML 4 there is no native slider, so if you just have some HTML elements (an <input>, some images) with some JavaScript attached to act and look like a slider. There is no way to tell the operating system that the role of this widget is a slider and what its current state and value are, and if the operating system doesn't know that vital information, assistive technology such as screen readers can't convey it to the user either.

NOTE If you start using these new ARIA attributes, you may notice that your HTML 4 pages won't validate anymore. As long as the rest of your markup is OK, that doesn't matter—accessibility trumps validity.

ARIA aims to bridge this situation by introducing a whole series of new attributes that browsers and assistive technologies can hook into.

So, using horrible old-school HTML you could—in theory—add ARIA to

```
<font size="+5" color="red">I should be a heading</font>
```

to make

```
<font size="+5" color="red" role="heading" aria-level="2">
¬I should be a heading</font>
```

This tells the user agent that this text is a heading, level 2. But of course, this would be nonsense, as HTML already has a perfectly valid and semantic way of defining this sort of structure with

```
<h2>I AM a heading</h2>
```

A developer might forget to bolt on the necessary ARIA attributes, whereas using the correct <h2> element has built-in "heading-ness" and built-in level so it's a lot more robust. ARIA is not a panacea or "get out of jail free" card for developers to start abusing markup and make everything out of <div>s and <span>s. Whenever possible, use the correct markup and only use ARIA for situations where the correct semantics can't be otherwise expressed (a slider in HTML 4 example, for instance).

The ARIA spec says "It is expected that, over time, host languages will evolve to provide semantics for objects that previously could only be declared with WAI-ARIA. When native semantics for a given feature become available, it is appropriate for authors to use the native feature and stop using WAI-ARIA for that feature."

So something like HTML5 <nav> shouldn't need ARIA role= navigation added to it, because it should (in an ideal world) have that built-in. However, HTML5 is very new, whereas ARIA already has some support in assistive technology. So it shouldn't hurt to use the built-in element *plus* the ARIA information, and it can only help users who rely on assistive technology. The HTML5 validator at **html5.validator.nu** therefore validates ARIA as well as HTML5 (whereas HTML 4 validators report ARIA information as an error because HTML 4 predates ARIA).

ARIA document structure and landmark roles

WAI-ARIA defines several roles that tell assistive technology about landmarks and structure of a document. Some of these are:

- application
- article
- banner
- complementary
- contentinfo
- document
- form
- heading
- main
- navigation
- search

Looking at a simple page from an ARIA perspective, you might see what is shown in **Figure 2.18**.

FIGURE 2.18 **A simple page with a header, sidebar, and main content area and ARIA roles.**

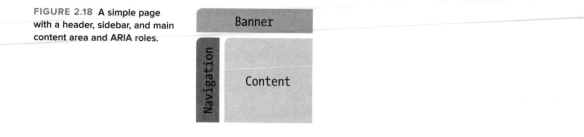

Some of these obviously match HTML5 elements, such as `<article>`, `<form>`, `<header>`, and `<nav>`.

Others do not have such an obvious one-to-one correspondence. For example, `role=banner` "typically includes things such as the logo or identity of the site sponsor, and site-specific search tool. A banner usually appears at the top of the page and typically spans the full width." That initially seems to match HTML5 `<header>`, but as you've seen, there can be multiple `<header>`s on a page. So the "page header" is the only one allowed to have `role=banner`.

Similarly, `contentinfo` is defined as "A large perceivable region that contains information about the parent document. Examples of information included in this region of the page are copyrights and links to privacy statements." This sounds like `<footer>`, but only the "page footer" and not each footer in a page with multiple footers.

`role=main` defines the "main content area" of a page. We discussed in Chapter 1 how that can be algorithmically deduced, but as assistive technologies can make use of ARIA *now*, it makes sense to add this role to the element you're using to group your main content. You can even use it as a hook for CSS in browsers that understand attribute selectors:

```
div[role=main] {color:red; background-color:yellow;
¬ font-family: "Comic Sans MS", cursive; ... }
```

There you have it: accessibility and gorgeous typography in perfect harmony.

Combining ARIA and HTML5

We recommend that you consider using ARIA where appropriate in addition to HTML5 as a transitional measure to improve accessibility that won't harm validation (but see the following note on screen readers). However, we don't do that in this book (as we're teaching you HTML5, not ARIA).

ARIA resources

There is a useful cross-reference in the spec of HTML5 and ARIA at **dev.w3.org/html5/spec/embedded-content-0.html#annotations-for-assistive-technology-products-aria**. Steve Faulkner of The Paciello Group has a list of ARIA information that is *not* built-in to HTML5 at **www.paciellogroup.com/blog/?p=585**.

A note on screen readers

Houston, we have a problem.

In 2007, I was concerned that no screen reader vendors were participating in the HTML5 specification process, so I wrote to the W3C to ask it to invite vendors to join. In 2009, I asked the HTML editor Ian Hickson if any responded. He replied "A couple did, but only to say they had little time for the standards process, which was quite disappointing. Since then, though, Apple has ramped up their efforts on their built-in Mac OS X screen reader software, and we do get a lot of feedback from Apple. So at least one screen reader vendor is actively involved."

A recent test (**www.accessibleculture.org/html5-aria/index.html**) shows that two of the largest commercial screen readers cannot properly process content that is marked up with *both* HTML5 and ARIA (oh, the irony) or in `<nav>` elements inside a `<header>`. Not all screen readers misbehave, however; Apple VoiceOver does not omit content, and the open-source NVDA screen reader (**www.nvda-project.org/**) speaks all content *and* allows navigation by ARIA landmarks.

Personally, I feel that if you are using the specification the right way, it is not your problem if a browser or screen reader cannot adequately deal with that content. However, that's my personal opinion; you might feel differently, or the legal situation where you are might require you to dumb down your code to accommodate those screen readers. Of course, they might fix the bugs by the time you read this book. In the meantime: **it's your responsibility to know your users and the law in your area.**

For more information on ARIA in general, see Gez Lemon's Introduction to WAI-ARIA **dev.opera.com/articles/view/introduction-to-wai-aria/** and follow The Paciello Group's blog (**www.paciellogroup.com/blog/**). Two recommended books are *Universal Design for Web Applications* by Wendy Chisholm and Matt May (O'Reilly) and *Designing with Progressive Enhancement: Building the Web that Works for Everyone* by Todd Parker et al (New Riders) for useful information on practical uses of ARIA.

The ARIA spec itself is at **www.w3.org/WAI/PF/aria/**.

Even more new structures!

You ain't seen nothing yet. Actually, that's untrue: you've seen loads already. So while we're in the zone, let's look at other new elements that HTML5 provides us, some of the changes from HTML4. We'll look at global attributes allowed on any element, as well as wave "hi" to a few HTML5 features that we won't cover in this book.

`<aside>`

In Chapter 1 you saw `<aside>` used to mark up sidebars. It represents "a section of a page that consists of content that is tangentially related to the content around the aside element, and which could be considered separate from that content. Such sections are often represented as sidebars in printed typography. The element can be used for typographical effects like pull quotes or sidebars, for advertising, for groups of nav elements, and for other content that is considered separate from the main content of the page."

Using an `<aside>` inside an `<article>`, for example, is the right place for tangentially related information or pull quotes about that article, but not, we hasten to add, page-wide navigation.

`<aside>` has an implied ARIA role of "note", but can be given `role="complementary"` or (if it surrounds a search form) `role="search"`.

`<details>`

I'm very fond of the `<details>` element, even though it has no implementations yet. However, Remy has a clever script that fakes it at **http://gist.github.com/370590**.

It's cool because it introduces native support for a common behaviour, removing the need for custom JavaScript (or, something I've seen on far too many sites to be funny, pulling in the full jQuery library). `<details>` provides an expanding/collapsing area. It takes the following form

```
<details>
 <summary>Photograph details</summary>
 <p>Photograph taken on <time datetime=2009-12-25>Xmas
 ¬ Day 09</time> with a Canon IXUSi.</p>
 <p><small>Copyright Bruce Lawson,
 ¬ <address>bruce@brucelawson.co.uk</address></small>.</p>
</details>
```

The contents of the descendent `<summary>` element are focusable and act as a control that, when activated by mouse or keyboard, expand or collapse the remainder of the element. If no `<summary>` element is found, the browser supplies its own default control text, such as "details" or a localised version. Browsers will probably add some kind of icon to show that the text is "expandable" such as a down arrow.

`<details>` can optionally take the open attribute to ensure that the element is open when the page is loaded:

`<details open>`

Note that the element isn't restricted to purely textual markup—it could be a login form, an explanatory video, a table of source data for a graph, or a description of the structure of a table for users who use assistive technology, have learning disabilities, or who (like me) simply don't "get" numbers.

`<figure>`

I've always felt a bit semantically grubby when adding a caption to a picture to explain the image or to give attribution to the photographer, because the only way to do it has been with text that runs into surrounding content, with no way to explicitly associate it with the image. There simply haven't been any markup constructs for this before. Perhaps I'm just weird, but that's why I'm very glad to see the `<figure>` element that wraps an image (or a video, or block of code, or a supporting quotation) and its caption, which goes in the `<figcaption>` element:

```
<figure>
<img src=welcome.jpg
   alt=""> <!-- no alt, as it's covered by the figcaption -->
<figcaption>
Bruce and Remy welcome questions
<small>Photo &copy; Bruce's mum</small>
</figcaption>
</figure>
```

Styling this markup can produce some nice effects (**Figure 2.19**).

Note that `<figcaption>` can only contain "phrasing content"—in HTML4 terms, it can't contain "block-level" elements.

FIGURE 2.19 `<figure>` and `<figcaption>` elements with some CSS3 designer bling. (Hey, this is a caption for a figure that's illustrating captions and figures. Now *that's* what I call "meta".)

Bruce and Remy welcome questions
Photo © Bruce's mum

HTML5 element categories and content models

HTML4 had divided elements into "block-level" and "inline." These names are gone from HTML5, as they're inherently presentational: They simply reflect the way browsers display them—with their default style sheets. There is nothing inherent to any HTML element that is "block" or "inline."

By default, CSS defines every element as `display:inline` until it's overridden by the browser's default style sheet or the gorgeous design that the sublimely talented designer that you are applies to the markup. (Don't blush, you know you are; everybody says so.)

In HTML5, meet lots of new content models, including *phrasing* (broadly equivalent to inline) and *flow* (broadly equivalent to block-level). Some (`<a>`, `<ins>`, `<del>`) can be both. Some content types (*heading* content like `<h1>..<h6>`, *sectioning* elements like `<article>`, `<section>`, `<nav>`, `<aside>`) are subsets of these.

There's also *embedded* (content that imports another resource into the document, or content from another vocabulary that is inserted into the document such as `<audio>`, `<canvas>`, `<embed>`, `<iframe>`, `<img>`, `<math>`, `<object>`, `<svg>`, `<video>`), *interactive* (`<a>`, `<audio>` (if the controls attribute is present), `<button>`, `<details>`, `<embed>`, `<iframe>`, `<img>` (if the usemap attribute is present), `<input>` (if the type attribute is not in the hidden state), `<keygen>`, `<label>`, `<menu>` (if the type attribute is in the toolbar state), `<object>` (if the usemap attribute is present), `<select>`, `<textarea>`, `<video>` (if the controls attribute is present), *metadata*, and others.

Don't get hung up on these. They're pretty intuitive: Apart from the fact that `<a>` now behaves like `<ins>` and `<del>` and can be "inline" or "block," you won't notice anything different from before if you're using the html5 shiv (**http://code.google.com/p/html5shiv/**) to define the new HTML5 elements until browsers define them in their style sheets.

<mark>

The `<mark>` element allows you to do the markup equivalent of using a highlighter pen to bring out some words on a printed page. It's not the same as emphasis—for that you use `<em>`. But if you had some existing text and wanted to bring something to the fore that isn't emphasised in the text, you could use `<mark>` and style it to be italics, or with a yellow highlighter-pen background colour. In print, you'll often see the phrases "my italics" or "emphasis added".

The spec also says "When used in the main prose of a document, it indicates a part of the document that has been highlighted due to its likely relevance to the user's current activity."

As an illustration, on my own site, I use an adapted version of Stuart Langridge's Searchhi script (**www.kryogenix.org/code/browser/searchhi/**), which checks to see if the referrer to a page was a search engine and the search terms are in the query string. If they are, the script walks the DOM and surrounds each instance of a search term with a `<mark>` element, which is then styled a pretty pink. It would have been wrong to wrap these search terms in `<strong>` or `<em>` as they're not emphatic—and this would have changed the meaning of the content of our page—but are relevant to the user's current activity: arriving at a page on our site looking for information about a certain search term.

`<ruby>`, `<rp>`, `<rt>`

ruby is a useful addition for those writing content in some Asian languages. Daniel Davis has a very useful article, "The HTML5 `<ruby>` element in words of one syllable or less" (**http://my.opera. com/tagawa/blog/the-html5-ruby-element-in-words-of-one-syl- lable-or-less**), in which he explains how it works in the context of Japanese (quoted with kind permission):

Any piece of Japanese text (banner ad, article, legal doc, and so on) uses a combination of kanji, hiragana, and katakana writing systems. It is sometimes the case that people reading the text can't read the kanji, especially because kanji characters can have more than one pronunciation. People and place names are one example of kanji having numerous or irregular pronunciations.

日 can be pronounced "nichi," "hi," or "ka"

本 can be pronounced "hon" or "moto"

日本 can be pronounced "nihon" or "nippon"

To help the reader, sometimes the pronunciation is written above the kanji using the hiragana alphabet. This is called *furigana* in Japanese and *ruby* in English (from the name of the small 5.5pt type size used for similar sorts of annotations in British print tradition). It is often used in newspapers and books but not so much on websites, due to the difficulty of squeezing miniature text above larger text on a single line. The `<ruby>` element aims to solve this.

According to the current HTML5 spec, the `<ruby>` element is an inline element and is placed around the word or character you'd like to clarify, like so:

```
<ruby>日本</ruby>
```

By itself this does nothing, so you add the pronunciation either for each character or, as in this case and our personal preference, for the word as a whole. For this, you use the `<rt>` tag, meaning ruby text.

`<ruby>日本<rt>にほん</rt></ruby>`

You could leave it like that and supporting browsers would show the hiragana pronunciation above the kanji text, but nonsupporting browsers would ignore the tags and show both the text and its pronunciation side by side. To solve this, you have another tag, `<rp>`, meaning ruby parentheses, which cleverly hides characters (namely parentheses) in supporting browsers. This means you can write the pronunciation in parentheses, which nonsupporting browsers will show, and supporting browsers will continue to show the pronunciation without parentheses above the main text (**Figure 2.20**).

`<ruby>日本<rp>(</rp><rt>にほん</rt><rp>)</rp></ruby>`

FIGURE 2.20 **In supporting browsers, ruby text is shown above main text. In nonsupporting browsers, ruby text is shown next to main text but in parentheses.**

にほん	
日本	日本 (にほん)
supporting browser	non-supporting browser

At time of writing, the `<ruby>` element is discussed a lot in the W3C HTML5 Japanese Interest group, so the spec is liable to change based on that feedback.

Redefined elements

HTML5 redefines some existing elements as well as adding new ones. Here are some old friends: some have radically changed, others have simply finessed their hairstyles.

<ol>

In HTML 4, the `start` attribute on `<ol>` was deprecated, as it was deemed presentational. Luckily, HTML5 reverts this wrong decision. If you want an ordered list to start at five rather than line one, use:

`<ol start=5>`

Something nice that isn't yet implemented in any browser is the reversed attribute. Consider the following example:

```
<h3>Top five dreamy mega-hunks</h3>
<ol reversed>
 <li>Brad Pitt</li>
 <li>George Clooney</li>
 <li>Orlando Bloom</li>
 <li>Remy Sharp</li>
 <li>Bruce Lawson</li>
</ol>
```

This creates a list that counts down from five (Mr. Pitt) to one (me). Sorry, Brad, George, and Orlando—but what do you guys know about HTML5?

<dl>

In HTML 4, <dl> was a definition list containing a term and one or more definitions for that term. This definition was muddy and confused, as it also mentioned the potential use of <dl> to mark up dialogues. It was regularly misused to mark up any name and value pairs regardless of whether one *defined* the other.

HTML5 widens the element to be "an association list consisting of zero or more name-value groups... Name-value groups may be terms and definitions, metadata topics and values, or any other groups of name-value data." Here's an example listing the books in Remy's collection, using <dt> and <dd> to group title and author(s).

```
<dl>
  <dt>Directory of French plastic sandal manufacturers</dt>
  <dd>Phillipe Philloppe</dd>
  <dt>J-Lo's plastic surgery: a profile</dt>
  <dd>Hugh Jarce</dd>
  <dt>The Orpheus and Eurydice myth</dt>
  <dd>Helen Bach</dd>
  <dt>The Proctologist and the Dentist</dt>
  <dd>Ben Dover</dd>
  <dd>Phil McCavity</dd>
</dl>
```

\<cite\>

In HTML 4, the `<cite>` element could be used to mark up the name of a speaker:

```
As <CITE>Harry S. Truman</CITE> said,<Q lang="en-us">
¬ The buck stops here.</Q>
```

HTML5 disallows this: "A person's name is not the title of a work— even if people call that person a piece of work— and the element must therefore not be used to mark up people's names."

This is bonkers. It makes existing content that conforms to the rules of HTML 4 nonconforming to the rules of HTML5, although it will never be flagged as invalid by a validator, as a machine has no way of knowing that "Harry S. Truman" is a name rather than the title of a biography called "Harry S. Truman."

In his 24ways.org article, "Incite a riot", Jeremy Keith wrote "Join me in a campaign of civil disobedience against the unnecessarily restrictive, backwards-incompatible change to the cite element."

I agree. Use `<cite>` for names if you want to.

\<address\>

`<address>` is for contact details of the author of the current `<article>` or document, *not* as a generic element for postal addresses. The contact details can be email address, postal address, or any others. These can be marked up as a microformat, RDFa, or microdata if you wish.

What's new is that you can have multiple addresses in a document, one inside each `<article>`. Author information associated with an `<article>` element does not apply to nested article elements, so a blog post in an `<article>` can have an `<address>` for its author, and each blog comment (which you remember is a nested `<article>`) can have the `<address>` of its commenter.

\<em\>, \<i\>

em marks up emphasis of the kind that subtly changes the meaning of a sentence; if the question is "Did you say you live in Paris?" the answer might be marked up as

```
<p>No, my <em>name</em> is Paris. I live in <em>Troy</em>.
¬ Cloth-ears.</p>
```

If you have relative levels of importance, you can nest em elements to make the contents extra emphatic.

The <i> element "represents a span of text in an alternate voice or mood, or otherwise offset from the normal prose, such as a taxonomic designation, a technical term, an idiomatic phrase from another language, a thought, a ship name, or some other prose whose typical typographic presentation is italicized."

Here are some examples of <i> where <em> would *not* be appropriate:

```
<p>The <i>Titanic</i> sails at dawn.</p>
<p>The design needs a bit more <i lang=fr>ooh la la</i>.</p>
<p>You, sir, deserve a jolly good kick up the <i>gluteus
maximus</i>!</p>
```

<strong>, <b>

The strong element represents strong importance for its contents but, unlike <em>, it does not change the meaning of the sentence. For example,

```
<p><strong>Warning! This banana is dangerous.</strong></p>
```

You can nest strong elements to make them extra-important.

The <b> element "represents a span of text to be stylistically offset from the normal prose without conveying any extra importance, such as key words in a document abstract, product names in a review, or other spans of text whose typical typographic presentation is boldened."

For example:

```
<p>Remy never forgot his fifth birthday—feasting on
¬ <b>powdered toast</b> and the joy of opening his gift:
¬ a <b>Log from Blammo!</b>.</p>
```

<hr>

The <hr> element is now media-independent and indicates "a paragraph-level thematic break." A comment on HTML5doctor put it nicely: It's the markup equivalent of the "* * *" that is often used in stories and essays. We were about to write it off as a historical curiosity when fellow Doctor Oli Studholme wrote "<hr> is used as a section separator quite frequently in Japanese design. They're generally hidden via CSS but visible when viewed on cHTML cell phone browsers, which only support very basic CSS and don't get the visual design (and with it the visual separation of sections)."

Our advice: use sectioning content and headings instead with CSS for pretty dividers.

<small>

The `<small>` element has been completely redefined, from simply being a generic presentational element to make text appear smaller to actually represent "small print," which "typically features disclaimers, caveats, legal restrictions, or copyrights. Small print is also sometimes used for attribution, or for satisfying licensing requirements."

If the whole page is a "legalese" page, don't use `<small>`. In that case, the legal text *is* the main content, so there is no need to use an element to differentiate the legalese. It's only for short runs of text. `<small>` has no bearing on `<strong>` or `<em>` elements.

Removed elements

Some elements you may know from HTML4 have been made completely obsolete in HTML5, such as `<applet>` (use `<embed>` instead), `<big>`, `<blink>`, `<center>`, `<font>`, and `<marquee>`. They will not validate and must not be used by authors. Frames are gone (but `<iframe>` remains). Good riddance.

HTML5 browsers must still render these dear departed elements, of course, as there are plenty of them still out there in the wild. But you must avoid them as if they were tarantulas, zombies, man-eating tigers, plutonium sandwiches, or Celine Dion songs.

Global attributes

There are also several new global attributes, which can be added to any element. They are covered in this section.

contenteditable

Invented by Microsoft, and reverse-engineered and implemented by all other browsers, contenteditable is now officially part of HTML.

contenteditable means two things for browsers: first, that users can edit the contents of elements with this attribute, so the element must be selectable and the browser must provide a caret to mark the current editing position; second, that changes made to the document affect the selected content specifically selected and editable, that is you can make the text bold, change the font, add lists, headings, and so on. contenteditable is a Boolean attribute, so it can be set to true or false. Although markup capitalisation is irrelevant, the DOM attribute requires contentEditable (note the capital *E*) . The DOM also has isContentEditable to assess whether this element is editable—since the contenteditable flag could have been inherited from a parent element.

You can also set document.designMode = 'on' (notice, not 'true') to enable the entire document to be editable. This can only be done using JavaScript.

Finally, any selected (that is, highlighted) content by the user can have a number of commands run against it, such as document.execCommand('bold'). Typical keyboard commands to make text bold or italic affect the DOM in the editable element.

If you want to use contenteditable for some form of CMS, you will want to save the changes to your server at some point. There's no particular API method for doing this, but since your user's changes have modified the DOM, you need to send the innerHTML of the editable element (or entire document if using designMode) back to the server for saving in your CMS.

contextmenu

contextmenu is related to <menu>, <command> which are not appearing in this book (see the section "Features not covered in this book").

data-*

You can pass information to scripts from markup using the data-* attribute. It can be any XML-compatible name. See Chapter 4 for an explanation.

draggable

draggable indicates that the element can be dragged using the drag-and-drop API (see Chapter 8).

hidden

This attribute is analogous to aria-hidden, which tells the browser that the content of this element shouldn't be rendered in any way. It doesn't only hide the content, but keeps it "in the wings," so that for instance you could use JavaScript later on to remove the attribute and cause the element to "pop" into being.

Quoting the specification (rather than attempting to paraphrase it any further): "The hidden attribute must not be used to hide content that could legitimately be shown in another presentation. For example, it is incorrect to use hidden to hide panels in a tabbed dialog, because the tabbed interface is merely a kind of overflow presentation—one could equally well just show all the form controls in one big page with a scrollbar. It is similarly incorrect to use this attribute to hide content just from one presentation—if something is marked hidden, it is hidden from all presentations, including, for instance, screen readers."

Even if you know that you'll be "unhiding" stuff later with some scripting, you should treat hidden stuff as if it literally wasn't there. So don't add links pointing to content that's hidden and don't tie other elements to it with aria-describedby or aria-labelledby.

item, itemprop, subject

These attributes are associated with the microdata specification (see the section "Features not covered in this book"), which this book doesn't cover.

role, aria-* attributes

As you've seen, HTML5 treats WAI-ARIA as legal additions to the language.

spellcheck

This Boolean attribute tells the browser to check the element's spelling and grammar. If it's missing, "the default state indicates that the element is to act according to a default behavior, possibly based on the parent element's own spellcheck state."

tabindex (=-1)

tabindex is a largely archaic concept that allows you to specify the order in which elements are focused when the user navigates a page with the keyboard (traditionally using the Tab key, though some browsers—most notably Opera—may use different key combinations for this).

This used to be quite popular when sites were built using deeply nested layout tables, but nowadays this is not usually necessary. The default tab order is determined by the order in which elements appear in your markup, so a properly ordered and structured document should never require additional tabbing hints.

However, tabindex does have a useful side-effect. Normally, only links, form elements, and image map areas can be focused via the keyboard. Adding a tabindex can make other elements also focusable, so executing a focus() command from JavaScript would move the browser's focus to them. However, this would also make these elements keyboard-focusable, which may not be desirable.

Using a negative integer (by convention, tabindex=-1) allows the element to be focused programmatically, "but should not allow the element to be reached using sequential focus navigation."

It's very useful in overcoming a bug in Internet Explorer whereby, under some circumstances, elements such as headings that were targets of in-page links were never focused for screen reader users, leaving the information inaccessible. (See **www.juicystudio. com/article/ie-keyboard-navigation.php** for more information.) In HTML 4, "`-1`" was an invalid value for the attribute, and the attribute itself was invalid on any element other than form fields and links. However, as it works in browsers now and it solves a real problem, HTML5 legalises it everywhere. Yay!

Features not covered in this book

For completeness, here are some of the most interesting features of HTML5 that, for reasons of page count or lack of implementation, aren't discussed further.

<embed>

`<embed>` is well-known and has been used for years, but was always an outlaw element that never validated. But like that other outlaw, Robin Hood, it was widely supported because it performed a useful function: It's the only way to get plug-ins such as Flash to work reliably in all browsers, which explains its overwhelmingly common usage (see 2008 stats at **http://dev.opera.com/articles/view/mama-plug-ins/**). Because of this, there's no reason to keep it from validating. HTML5 paves that particular cowpath and finally includes it into the formal language specification.

But hang on. Isn't HTML5 supposed to replace all these plug-in-based technologies? Contrary to the sensationalist headlines of some journalists, HTML5 won't magically replace plug-ins overnight, and now we can embed them into HTML5 without incurring the wrath of the validator.

<keygen>

This element, which is already well supported in all browsers other than the big IE elephant in the room, is used in situations where your form needs to send a public key. If you

don't know what public-key cryptography is, take a look at
http://en.wikipedia.org/wiki/Public_key.

And if you're still lost, you don't actually need this element!

<progress>, <meter>

`<progress>` is used to represent a "progress meter," to indicate
the completion of a task—downloading a file, for example.

`<meter>` "represents a scalar measurement within a known range,
or a fractional value; for example disk usage, the relevance of
a query result, or the fraction of a voting population to have
selected a particular candidate."

<menu>, <command>

These are exciting elements that allow you to define toolbars or
context menus for your application, with icons and associated
commands that execute scripts when activated. They're cooler
than a bucket full of Lou Reeds. However, no browser yet supports them, so we don't discuss them further.

microdata

Microdata is a method of marking up elements with additional
machine-readable data, so that crawlers, search engines, or
browsers can extract information from the page. It's similar to
RDFa (a W3C standard) and microformats (a popular set of con-
ventions), and is already indexed by the Google search engine if
used in markup. However, no browser supports its associated API.

<style scoped>

The scoped attribute on a style element tells the browser
to apply the styles to the element that the `<style scoped>`
element is in, and its children. This allows for highly localised
styling right inside your HTML, an `<article>` that contains a
scoped style block can be syndicated and retain its special
styles, for instance.

However, no browser supports it yet.

Summary

Phew, that was quite a ride, wasn't it? You've seen a lot of new structures, new elements, and quite a few changes to existing elements. If you've studied our markup examples carefully, you also know the favoured weaponry of fairies, so beware if you're a goblin or an orc.

HTML5 allows us to mark up common website structures with dedicated elements, rather than empty <div> or <span> elements. These are still completely necessary parts of the language. Just as with HTML 4, you should use these generic containers when there aren't any more appropriate elements, but now you have a larger arsenal of elements to choose from. You've also seen that some of these new elements have conceptually built-in roles to help assistive technologies. However, while we're in this transitional period and browser (and more importantly screen reader) support for these built-in roles may still be lacking, you can still (validly and legally) add extra ARIA information.

It probably seems pretty complex, but take my word for it: as you use these new constructs, they soon become much easier to understand. The only way to familiarise yourself with these new constructs is to start using them, so get stuck in!

CHAPTER 3

Forms

Bruce Lawson

ONE OF THE problems with HTML 4 forms is that they're just dumb fields. Validation is required on the server, of course, but you have to duplicate it in the user's browser with JavaScript to give them the seamless experience they deserve. Given that almost every Web page has some kind of form—search, comments forms, sign-up, etc.—wouldn't it be great if browsers had built-in validation for some of the most common data types that we collect?

You guessed it: HTML5 forms provide exactly that.

We ♥ HTML, and now it ♥s us back

HTML5 makes developing forms quicker. There are some nice goodies like the addition of two HTTP types of form action (update and delete) to go with the current get and post.

More sexily, a number of elements that were previously required to be within a form element (`<button>`, `<fieldset>`, `<input>`, `<label>`, `<select>`, `<textarea>`, plus `<object>` and the new elements like `<keygen>`, `<meter>`, `<output>`, and `<progress>`) can be anywhere on the page and associated with a form using a form attribute pointing at the id of its *form owner*.

Consider this example:

```
<form id=foo>
<input type="text">
...
</form>
<textarea form=foo></textarea>
```

The `<input>` is owned by the form foo, as it is contained within it and it does not have a form attribute overriding that ownership. The `<textarea>` is outside the form, but is still owned by it, as its form attribute points to the id of its form owner.

This gives a lot more flexibility with styling when you want those elements to appear visually (and structurally) outside the parent forms.

But the big wins are the new HTML5 form types and the built-in validation that they bring. Eventually, you won't need JavaScript validation at all for these fundamental data types, although you can't mothball your scripts yet—the new input types degrade gracefully but will need your JavaScript until the golden future when everyone has an HTML5 browser (or your boss tells you that users of ancient browsers will just have to put up with server-side-only form checking).

New input types

The new form fields were the genesis of the spec that became HTML5, and it's where we see the backwards-compatible extension principle in action. The extensions are largely new values of the type attribute of the input element. As all browsers default to <input type=text>, legacy browsers that don't understand the new extensions will fall back to the default and allow the user to enter data in a plain text field.

> **NOTE** The specification makes no requirements on how browsers should present the new input types to the user or report errors, etc. Different browsers and different devices will present different user interfaces; compare, for example, the different ways that a select box is shown on Safari on desktop and Safari/iPhone (**Figure 3.1**).

FIGURE 3.1 The same select box rendered in Safari/Windows (left) and Safari/iPhone. Most screenshots are from Opera, as that has the most complete implementation at time of writing (May 2010), but where something is implemented in another browser, we use that instead.

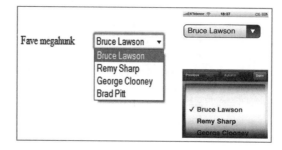

The email input type

The markup <input type=email> tells the browser that it should not allow the form to be submitted if the user has not entered what looks like a valid email address—that is, it doesn't check whether the email address exists or not, only whether it's in a valid format. As with all input types, the user may submit the form with this field empty unless the required attribute is present.

The manner in which the browser reports errors is not defined. The (experimental) implementation in Opera 10.50 is shown in **Figure 3.2**.

FIGURE 3.2 An automatically generated error message in Opera 10.50.

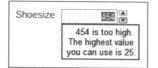

The multiple attribute is allowed, which means that the value of the field can be a list of comma-separated valid email addresses. Of course, this does not require that the user enter a comma-separated list manually; a browser may perfectly well pop up a list of the user's contacts from his mail client or phone contacts list, with checkboxes.

The experimental Firefox Contacts addon **http://mozillalabs. com/blog/2010/03/contacts-in-the-browser** collects contacts from various sources, which it uses to offer addresses when a user comes across an `<input type=email>`. It also exposes this contact information to website scripts through the W3C draft Contacts API (**http://www.w3.org/2009/dap/**).

The URL input type

`<input type=url>` causes the browser to ensure that the entered field is a correct URL. A browser may offer assistance to the user— for example, Opera shows a list of recently visited URLs from the user's browsing history and automatically prepends "http://" to URLs beginning with "www." (A URL need not be a web URL; the page could, for example, be a web-based HTML editor in which the user may wish to use the `tel:` pseudo-protocol.)

The date input type

The `date` type is one of my favourites. We've all seen web pages that require the user to enter a date for a flight, concert ticket, etc. Because dates are tricky to enter (is the format DD-MM-YYYY or MM-DD-YYYY or DD-MMM-YY?), developers code JavaScript date picker widgets that vary wildly in appearance, usability, and accessibility between sites.

`<input type=date>` solves this problem. Opera, for example, pops up a calendar widget (**Figure 3.3**).

On the BlackBerry browser in BlackBerry Device Software version 5.0, the date input control used to implement the date input field is the same Java component used within the native BlackBerry calendar app (although it isn't integrated with the calendar app). See **Figure 3.4**.

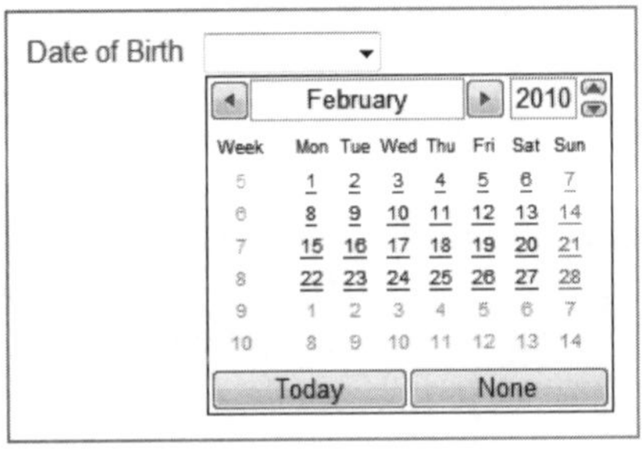

FIGURE 3.3 Opera 10.50 renders a calendar widget.

FIGURE 3.4 `<input type=date>` on the BlackBerry browser.

Of course, these are early days. The browser could call up the native calendar application so you could browse dates to see your prior appointments. The point is that the browser can now understand what you mean. Previously, date pickers were—from the perspective of the browser—nothing more than <div>s, <span>s, and links with lots of JavaScript behaviour attached. Now the browser knows that you're in fact entering an actual time and date and can offer richer controls and integration with other time/date information.

The time input type

<input type=time> allows input of a time in 24-hour format and validates it. Once again, the actual user interface is left to the browser; it could be as simple as entering numbers and throwing an error if the user enters an hour greater than 24 or minute greater than 59, or it could be far more elaborate: a clock face, for example, with draggable hands. The user interface can also allow for entry of a time zone offset.

The datetime input type

date and time validate a precise date and time. Local date and time works as datetime except that the browser doesn't allow the user to add (or change) a time zone offset.

The month input type

<input type=month> allows entry and validation of a month. Although internally this is stored as a number between 1 and 12, the browser may offer a selection method that uses the names of the months instead. You could do this with a select box with 12 options, January to December, but this doesn't localise. Using an HTML5 month input type, a French-localisiation of a browser could offer a drop-down with "Janvier" instead of January, for example. That's more work for the browser *and less work for you,* and that's the way it should be.

The week input type

`<input type=week>` allows entry and validation of a week number. While this could be a simple input field allowing a user to input a number, it's more complex in practice: some years have 53 weeks. Therefore, the format is 2010-W07 for the seventh week in the year 2010.

Opera offers a datepicker UI, which populates the input field with the week number of any selected date rather than the dates YYYY-MM-DD format (**Figure 3.5**).

FIGURE 3.5 **Opera 10.50's rendering of** `<input type=week>`.

week
2010-W06

◄	February	►	2010
Week	Mon	Tue	Wed	Thu	Fri	Sat	Sun
5	1	2	3	4	5	6	7
6	8	9	10	11	12	13	14
7	15	16	17	18	19	20	21
8	22	23	24	25	26	27	28
9	1	2	3	4	5	6	7
10	8	9	10	11	12	13	14

Today   None

The number input type

The `number` input type throws an error if the user does not enter numeric characters, unsurprisingly. It works perfectly with the `min`, `max`, and `step` attributes. In Opera, it is rendered as a spinner control that will not go beyond the upper and lower limits (if specified) and which progresses by the increment specified in `step`, although a user can also type the value (**Figure 3.6**).

FIGURE 3.6 **Opera 10.50's rendering of** `<input type=number>`.

The range input type

`<input type=range>` renders as a slider. **Figure 3.7** shows it in Google Chrome.

FIGURE 3.7 **Google Chrome's rendering of** `<input type=range>`.

Previously, sliders needed to be faked by hijacking an input and using JavaScript and images for the pointers. Because these were not native in the browser, great care needed to be taken—and extra code written—to ensure keyboard accessibility. Now that sliders are natively part of HTML, the responsibility is removed from the developer, leading to leaner code and greater accessibility for keyboard users.

See the example in the "Putting All This Together" section for more information.

The search input type

This input type expects a search term. In Safari there is also an unspecified attribute that adds a history of recent results, using the results=n attribute. The difference between search and text type is only stylistic, and in Safari on the Mac, it takes the operating system's default rounded-corners style for search—which can nonetheless be overwritten with some proprietary CSS (hat-tip to Wilfred Nas for this):

```
input[type="search"] {-webkit-appearance: textfield;}
```

The tel input type

The tel type expects a telephone number. There is no special validation; it doesn't even enforce numeric-only input, as many phone numbers are commonly written with extra characters, for example +44 (0) 208 123 1234.

As mobile phones "know" their own number, we expect that most mobile phones will be able to do things like autocompleting these entry fields. None currently does this, although the iPhone brings up a telephone number input screen (**Figure 3.8**).

FIGURE 3.8 The iPhone's keypad for completing
`<input type=tel>`.

The color input type

`<input type=color>` allows the user to input a colour value via a picker. So far, it's only implemented on the BlackBerry (**Figure 3.9**).

New attributes

As well as new input types, the `input` element has several new attributes to specify behaviour and constraints: autocomplete, min, max, multiple, pattern, and step. There's also a new attribute, list, that hooks up with a new element to allow a new data input method.

The list attribute

The `<datalist>` is reminiscent of a select box, but allows users to enter their own text if they don't want to choose one of the predefined options. The list is contained in a new `<datalist>` element, the id of which is referenced in the value of the list attribute:

```
<input id=form-person-title  type=text list=mylist>
    <datalist id=mylist>
        <option label=Mr value=Mr>
        <option label=Ms value=Ms>
        <option label=Prof value="Mad Professor">
    </datalist>
```

`<datalist>` has no rendering of its own, but instead shows up as values in a select-like field.

The previous example uses type=text to allow freeform input, but you can use `<datalist>` with any of the input types mentioned previously: for example, url, email, etc. It's possible also to dynamically repopulate the options as the user types, replicating the Google Suggest functionality. See **http://dev.opera.com/articles/view/an-html5-style-google-suggest/** for more details.

Many have asked why the `<input>`/`<datalist>` pair isn't combined into a single new element like `<select>` is. The answer lies with backwards compatibility: the `<input>`/`<datalist>` pairing degrades to `<input type=text>` in legacy browsers, so the user can at least enter something, and so you can easily fake the full implementation with JavaScript for those browsers as well.

The autofocus attribute

The autofocus Boolean provides a declarative way to focus a form control during page load. Previously, a developer needed to write JavaScript using `control.focus()`. The new way allows the browser to do clever things like not actually focusing the control if the user is already typing elsewhere (a common problem of old-school JavaScript onload focus scripts).

There should only be one such input field on a page. From a usability perspective, this attribute should be used with care. We recommend only using it on pages that have a form field as their central purpose—a search form, for example.

The placeholder attribute

A usability trick employed regularly by developers is placing text in an input field as a hint for the user, removing the text when the user focuses on the field, and restoring the text when focus leaves the field. This used to require JavaScript. However, it can now be done declaratively with the `placeholder` attribute. The specification says "For a longer hint or other advisory text, the `title` attribute is more appropriate."

When browsers need a helping hand

With older—and even some newer—browsers, some of these features aren't available natively. This isn't such a problem, though, as *most* of the new HTML5 features can be *patched* using JavaScript (or other technologies, like Flash and Silverlight) to bring the browser's support capability up to speed. This isn't graceful degradation nor progressive enhancement; it's something else. Something my colleagues and I are calling *polyfilling*, whereby we rely on native functionality in our code and then fill the gaps in support using an external library. That library may be generic or it may be specific. For example, if you want to make use of `autofocus` or the `placeholder` attribute, you can include a small JavaScript library, and all the current browsers now support these two attributes, ranging from IE6 to Firefox 3.6 (http://introducinghtml5.com/examples/ch03/polyfilling.html).

It is currently rendered by WebKit-based browsers (having originally been a proprietary Apple HTML extension) and an alpha version of Firefox 4 beta.

The required attribute

The new `required` attribute can be used on `<textarea>` and most input fields (except when the type attribute is hidden, image, or some button types such as submit). The browser will not allow the user to submit the form if required fields are empty. We recommend also adding the ARIA attribute `aria-required` to such input fields for assistive technology (see the discussion of ARIA in Chapter 2).

The multiple attribute

`<input type=file>` is not new in HTML5, but when used in conjunction with the new `multiple` attribute, the user can now upload multiple files:

`<input type=file multiple>`

It can also be used with any other input type: for example, `<input type=email multiple>` allows the user to enter multiple email addresses. Currently this is implemented only in WebKit browsers.

The pattern attribute

Some of the input types mentioned previously—email, number, url, etc.—are really "baked-in" regular expressions as the browser just checks if the values entered look like they should.

> **NOTE** If regular expressions scare you but you want to learn more, or you're keen to fuel your regular expression ninja skills, you can take a gander at Steven Levithan's blog, which almost exclusively talks about regular expressions: http://blog.stevenlevithan.com/

Suppose you want to match against a different tempate? The `pattern` attribute allows you to specify a custom regular expression that the input must match. So, if the user must always enter a single digit plus three uppercase alphabetic characters, the regular expression would be one number [0–9] and three letters [A–Z]{3}, all in uppercase, and the input would be coded:

```
<input pattern="[0-9][A-Z]{3}" name=part
        title="A part number is a digit followed by three
        ¬ uppercase letters.">
```

You could also add a placeholder="9AAA" or some such as a short hint.

The specification explains that the regular expressions in the pattern attribute match the syntax of regular expressions in JavaScript, except that there's an implied ^(:? at the beginning and)$ at the end.

So if you're accustomed to working with regular expressions, you're going to already be familiar with what you need to do. If not, you've got the fun world of regular expressions to explore!

The Internet is littered with JavaScript regular expressions that match this, that, and the other, so it's likely that you'll find what you're looking for. However, regular expressions, when kept simple, are relatively easy to get working.

For example, to match a ZIP code in the format of 99999 or 99999-9999 (assuming the 9s are all kinds of numbers), you can use:

```
<input pattern="[0-9]{5}(\-[0-9]{4})?" title="A zip code in
¬ the format of 99999 or 99999-9999">
```

This regular expression looks for a numerical sequence of five, with an optional suffix of a dash then another sequence of four numbers.

We could extend this match to also validate UK post codes (using a simplified post code match), by making the pattern more complicated:

```
<input required pattern="[0-9]{5}(\-[0-9]{4})?|[a-zA-Z]
¬ {1,2}\d{1,2}\s?\d[a-zA-Z]{1,2}" name=part title="A valid
¬ zip code or UK postcode">
```

Now our regular expression has become much more complicated and it can be quite tricky to test in the pattern. Since the pattern's regular expression matches the syntax of a JavaScript regular expression, we can test this in a browser console such as Firebug or Opera Dragonfly, using pure JavaScript to test whether the pattern is going to work. In the example below, I'm just testing the UK post code match, and using the JavaScript test method to experiment. Note that I've also wrapped my tests with the leading ^(:? and trailing)$ as the HTML5 spec states:

```
/^(:?[a-zA-Z]{1,2}\d{1,2}\s?\d[a-zA-Z]{1,2})$/.test
¬ ("bn14 8px")
> true
/^(:?[a-zA-Z]{1,2}\d{1,2}\s?\d[a-zA-Z]{1,2})$/.test
¬ ("bn149 8px")
> false
```

Those results are correct, since "bn149" isn't a legal part of a post code (or certainly not for this contrived example!). Finally, it's worth noting that the pattern attribute is case sensitive, and since we don't have any way to switch to case *insensitive* mode we need to explicitly match on lowercase and uppercase in this example.

The autocomplete attribute

Most browsers have some kind of autocomplete functionality. The new `autocomplete` attribute lets you control how this works.

The default state is for the input to inherit the autocomplete state of its form owner. Forms have autocomplete on by default.

If the autocomplete attribute of a form element is set to on, the field is fine for autocompletion.

I'll quote the wry humour of the specification's description of the off state: "The off state indicates either that the control's input data is particularly sensitive (for example, the activation code for a nuclear weapon); or that it is a value that will never be reused (for example, a one-time-key for a bank login) and the user will therefore have to explicitly enter the data each time."

The min and max attributes

As we've seen with `<input type=number>`, these attributes constrain the range of values that can be entered in an input; you can't submit the form with a number smaller than `min` or larger than `max`. But it can also be used with other input types—for example, `<input type=date min=2010-01-01 max=2010-12-31>` will not accept a date that's not in the year 2010. It's trivial to make the server write HTML that has a `min` of today, so only future days are allowed (for a flight booking site, for example) or a `max` of today (for a field collecting date of birth, for example).

The step attribute

`step` controls the level of granularity of input. So if you want the user to enter a percentage between 0 and 100, but only to the nearest 5, you can specify

`<input type=number mix=0 max=100 step=5>`

and the spinner control will increment in steps of 5.

Taking the example of a time control, you can also use `step=any`. This allows any time in the day to be selected, with any accuracy (for example, thousandth-of-a-second accuracy or more); normally, time controls are limited to an accuracy of one minute.

```
<input name=favtime type=time step=any>
```

Putting all this together

It's pretty confusing to work out which attributes go with which input types when you're meeting them all at once as we are here. But it's actually quite straightforward when you start using them. For example, you can't use `min` and `max` on a `<textarea>`, because that wouldn't make sense, but you can use `required`.

A blog comments form

Let's look at a classic form example that most of us will already be familiar with. Nearly all blogs have a comment section, with fields for commenter's name (required), her email address (required), URL (optional), and the comment (required). That would need a fair bit of JavaScript if we were to do our form validation by hand.

In HTML5, however, it requires only some new form types, each with a name attribute that the spec requires in order to participate in automatic validation. We also add a submit button—currently Opera only validates fields when a form is actually submitted, although the :invalid pseudo-class is applied as the user types.

```
<form>
  <label for=form-name>Name</label>
  <input name=form-name id=form-name type=text required>
  <label for=form-email>Email</label>
  <input name=form-email id=form-email type=email required>
  <label for=form-url>URL</label>
  <input name=form-url id=form-url type=url>
  <label for=form-comment>Comment</label>
  <textarea name=form-comment id=form-comment required>
  </textarea>
  <input type=submit>
</form>
```

Presto! No JavaScript is needed at all!

A slider, with scripted output

We've seen `<input type=range>`, so let's code up an example that actually shows the user the range allowed by the slider by automatically showing the minimum and maximum values, and dynamically outputting the current value of the slider.

The slider will go from 1 to 11, as all good controls should (be they for guitar amps or otherwise). The step will be 1, which is the default, so we can omit that attribute.

```
<input type=range min=1 max=11 name=tap>
```

To show the user the minimum and maximum values, we use generated content (which doesn't work on sliders in WebKit browsers):

```
input[type=range]::before {content: attr(min);}
input[type=range]::after {content: attr(max);}
```

This will show the values, and style them as defined in CSS. For example, **Figure 3.10** renders:

```
input[type=range]{width:500px; color:red; font-family:
¬cursive; font-size:2em;}
```

FIGURE 3.10 Opera's rendering of `<input type=range>` with `min` and `max` values generated.

We'll echo the current value of the slider with the new output element.

The <output> element

The `<output>` element is for showing results of some calculation or other with script. It can have a form owner, either by being inside a form or via a form attribute. The new `<progress>` and `<meter>` elements can be similarly associated with a form to provide feedback to a user.

We tie it to the slider by the name of the slider (name=tap), and the **onforminput** event. When the output's form owner receives input (as the slider is moved) we'll echo back the value of that input:

```
<output onforminput="value=tap.value">5</output>
```

The actual contents of the output element (in this case, "5") are only shown before the slider is changed. You should take care to ensure that this value is the same as any value attribute of the associated input field. In this example, the value=... part sets the visible value to whatever you set the slider to. This could be considered akin to this.innerHTML and value is just acting as a shortcut.

The output element can be styled with CSS (although currently it's only supported in Opera).

Using WAI-ARIA for transitional accessibility

Although we said that <input type=range> removed responsibility for accessibility from the developer, that's only true when HTML5 is widely supported and assistive technology understands this new type of form input.

During this transitional time, if you want to use HTML5 sliders, you should also add some WAI-ARIA information (which for the time being will result in some duplication):

```
<input id=tap
       name=tap
       type=range
       min=1
       max=10
       value=0
       role=slider
       aria-valuemin=1
       aria-valuemax=11
       aria-valuenow=0>
```

role=slider tells assistive technology how to map the control to operating system controls. You should update aria-valuenow with JavaScript when the slider position is changed. In this case you would want to bind to the change event on the slider; in our example we'll just use the onchange attribute. Unfortunately, we can't use the property syntax to update the aria-valuenow value; we have to update the DOM attribute for the value to update correctly:

```
<input id=tap
       name=tap
       type=range
       min=1
       max=10
       value=0
       role=slider
       aria-valuemin=1
       aria-valuemax=11
       aria-valuenow=0
       onchange="this.setAttribute('aria-valuenow',
       ¬this.value)">
```

This will update the value of the `aria-valuenow` attribute, and can be tested if you inspect the element using a DOM inspector.

Backwards compatibility with legacy browsers

> **NOTE** Alternatively, you can use the Modernizr library to do this work for you. Modernizr is a small library (currently 7K) that performs feature detection and returns JavaScript Booleans like `Modernizr.inputtypes[email]` set to true or false. There are some gotchas (watch out for WebKit!) but it's under active development. You can download it from **www.modernizr.com**.

The big question is: What can we do for legacy browsers? The answer is that you don't retire your pre-existing JavaScript validation just yet, but you leave it as a fallback after doing some feature detection. For instance, to detect whether `<input type=email>` is supported, you make a new `<input type=email>` with JavaScript, but don't add it to the page. Then, you interrogate your new element to find out what its type attribute is. If it's reported back as "email", then the browser supports the new feature—so let it do its work and don't bring in any JavaScript validation. If it's reported back as "text", it's fallen back to the default, indicating that it's not supported. So your code should load in an alternative validation library ideally through a *lazy load* technique so that by default, HTML5-aware browsers don't need to download and process JavaScript that isn't required.

```
var i = document.createElement("input");
i.setAttribute("type", "email");
return i.type !== "text";
```

You can test attributes, too:

```
return 'autofocus' in document.createElement("input");
```

Watch out for WebKit

It's worth noting that currently the desktop-based WebKit browsers, namely Safari and Chrome, both claim to support types: email, url, tel, and number using these detection methods. In fact, the live production browsers don't have this support as yet, and it's only reported this way because Mobile Safari (which is also WebKit) supports these input types to provide custom keyboards depending on the type (as shown on the iPhone in Figure 3.8). This is the browser providing device-specific support, typically via the keyboard (in particular on the iPhone), depending on the input type.

So what does this buy you? Well, first and foremost, you're future-proofing your code for that time when all browsers support these hugely useful additions to forms. Secondly, you buy a usability and accessibility win.

Styling new form fields and error messages

Whenever we present the new intelligent form fields at conferences, someone asks us how you can style these new fields. You can do some basic styling on most of the new controls: fonts, colours, and the like. Some aspects of the CSS Basic User Interface module (**http://www.w3.org/TR/css3-ui/**) apply to these elements—for example, the :invalid and :required pseudo-classes are applicable. But if you want to make all weekends in the date picker green, or make error messages purple, you can't. The selectors and CSS hooks for these parts of the new form controls haven't been specified yet.

This isn't a bad thing. Your branding people will, of course, lament that placeholder text isn't in corporate colours. But it's a usability and accessibility win. Although it's tempting to style the stuffing out of your form fields (which can, incidentally, lead to madness—see **http://meyerweb.com/eric/thoughts/2007/05/15/formal-weirdness/**), whatever your branding people say, it's better to leave forms as close to the browser defaults as possible. A browser's slider and date pickers will be the same across different sites, making it much more comprehensible to users. It's much better that a datepicker on site X looks and behaves the same as a datepicker on site Y or site Z.

And, by using native controls rather than faking sliders and date pickers with JavaScript, your forms are much more likely to be accessible to users of assistive technology.

Overriding browser defaults

When we make use of the new HTML5 form control types or the required attribute, the browser gives us pre-baked validation, with its own built-in error messages. That's great, but what if you want to customise these error messages? What if it's speak like a pirate day? Perhaps I want to change all the validation messages to speak like a pirate, too.

It's possible, with a bit of JavaScript. It's not possible to set custom validation messages using content attributes (which are hard-coded in the markup), but we can add them to the DOM attributes (which are accessible through JavaScript). So we can either set these before the validation runs, or when the form is submitted we can set a custom validation message and, at that point in execution, dynamically create a validation message that includes the value causing the error.

So instead of reading:

humptydumpty is not a legal e-mail address

We'll change the validation to read the following in "traditional" pirate speak:

humptydumpty be not *a legal e-mail address*

The setCustomValidity method allows me to specify my own validation message:

```
var email = document.getElementById('email');
email.form.onsubmit = function () {
  email.setCustomValidity(email.value + " be not a legal
  ¬ e-mail address");
};
```

You can see Opera rendering the custom validation message in **Figures 3.11** and **3.12**.

Opera is currently the only browser that has support for the native validation messages, and so there's nothing to benchmark against. I say this because you'll notice the custom validation message is prefixed with "The value humptydumpty is not allowed by a script on the page!". This is still in the browser's control, and we can do nothing to change this (at time of writing). So it's something to be wary of if you're going to use custom validation messages.

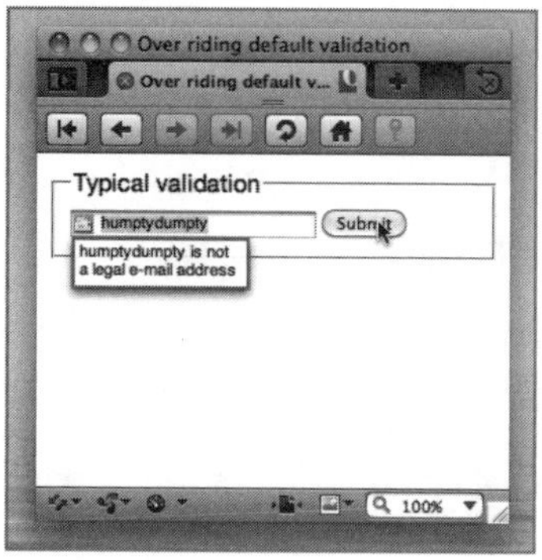

FIGURE 3.11 Opera rendering the default validation message for email.

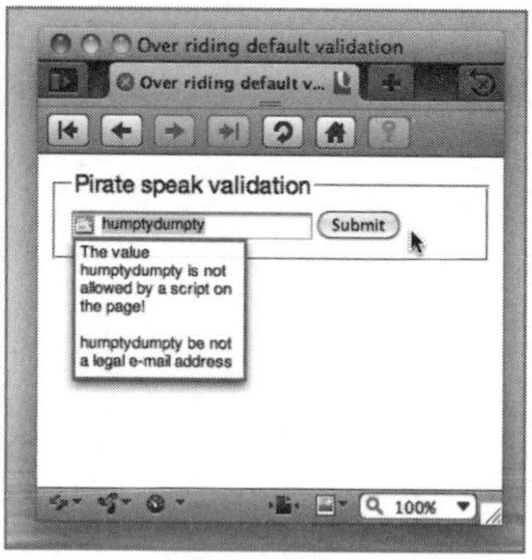

FIGURE 3.12 Opera rendering our custom "speak like a pirate day" validation.

However, if the way the custom validation messages work isn't your bag, then there is a way to roll your own validation behaviour, to make it feel more integral to your application. When we run `setCustomValidity` it sets the read-only DOM attribute called `validationMessage`. We can use this if we manage validation ourselves, which we'll look at in the next section.

Using JavaScript for DIY validation

Along with the content attributes that enable client-side validation and web form widget goodness, as with most of the HTML5 specs, there's an accompanying JavaScript API that gives us complete control over how our form is validated and submitted.

Using the JavaScript API we can control how we present validation feedback to our visitor, but we can still defer all the actual validation code to the new forms APIs. We can also use the API to narrow down exactly why a particular form field failed to validate.

Forcing element validation

All form elements and input elements (including `<select>` and `<textarea>`) include a `checkValidity` method on the DOM node. You'd be forgiven for thinking this is the method you'd want to use to override the browser's default validation and feedback process.

The `checkValidity` method returns true or false depending on the success of the validation checks, but at the same time it's *telling* the browser to run through its checks. If you want to take control of the presentation of validation feedback, then you *don't* want to use this method.

Element validity

Individual form fields, along with having the checkValidity method, also have a validity DOM attribute that returns a ValidityState object. There's a number of state attributes on the validity object, but the simplest and most important is the `valid` attribute. This value can be tested using JavaScript to drive a bespoke validation feedback system.

If we hook into the submit event handler on our form, we can manually loop through all the input fields and check the validity attribute. But what happens if the field *doesn't* have any validation rules? You're in luck: The API provides a willValidate attribute that we can test to see whether we should or shouldn't try to validate this particular field. Here's a (contrived) example:

```
var email = document.getElementById('email');
if (email.willValidate) {
  if (!email.validity.valid) {
    alert("Yarr, ye old email be invalid");
  }
}
```

Once you have the individual form field's validation state, you could pull in any custom messages set via element.validationMessage or test the different validity states, which also include valueMissing, typeMismatch, patternMismatch, tooLong, rangeUnderflow, rangeOverflow, stepMismatch, and customError.

Avoiding validation

The last question we need to answer is: What if you want to submit the form—but you *don't* want the browser to validate it? This is possible, too. But why on earth would you want to do this? What if you have a multi-stage registration form, either for sign-up or for submitting some content? For long forms it could be useful to split the form into stages (as eBay might do when you're selling an item). You might even want to allow your visitors to save the *state* of their submission, even if the form isn't currently complete and valid.

There are two levels of control for *not* validating. This can apply to the individual input control or to the entire form. The `novalidate` attribute can only be set on a form element and prevents validation for that particular field. So far there's no practical use case for this field, only theoretical ones. For example, you might be in the situation where you want to use type="email", and perhaps with browsers from the future will accept type="email" that allows the user to perform a lookup from their address book. But you're not bothered about actually validating any manual input the user might make—for instance, because their email is part of an intranet, and doesn't look like your typical email address. Using the `novalidate` attribute on the form element allows you to achieve this.

The second method, `formnovalidate`, which is practical and available today, is allowed on individual input elements and button elements (though probably only makes sense on type="submit" and type="button"). The `formnovalidate` attribute allows the form to be submitted and bypass all the validation that has been set on the form fields. The following example snippet of code would allow you to have a "save session" button with each fieldset to allow the user to save his progress without triggering the validation rules from running until he hits the final submit button:

```
<form>
  <fieldset>
    <legend>Some bits about you</legend>
    <div>
      <label for="email">Email:</label>
      <input id="email" name="email" type="email" required />
    </div>
    <div>
      <label for="url">Homepage:</label>
      <input id="url" type="url" name="url" />
    </div>
    <input type="submit" value="save session"
    ¬ formnovalidate />
  </fieldset>
```

You could even hook into the "save session" button to trigger JavaScript-based validation based on only those fields inside the fieldset via the `HTMLFieldSetElement.elements` property (though this is a new property in the HTML5 spec, so you may have to rely on `fieldset.getElementsByTagName` and find all the form fields).

The "whenever anything changes" event

One almost insignificant change to the <form> element is a new event called oninputchange. In fact, this a useful event that fires on the form element when any of the form fields within the form change. This saves you having to attach lots of onchange handlers to each form control.

For instance, if I were to create a colour picker that gives me both RGBA and HSLA, typically I would have to hook event listeners to each of the value sliders, but by using the oninputchange event, I'm able to hook a single event listener to the form and recalculate my RGBA and HSLA values using a single method.

The result, whether I'm attaching lots of event listeners or just a single one, is very similar. However, this feels a lot cleaner and better designed, as there's no duplication of event hooking.

When a slider is changed, it will generate the RGBA and HSLA and update the preview colour. The code listing below is just the JavaScript required:

```
form.onforminput = function () {
  var i = this.length, values = [], value = 0;
  while (i--, value = this[i].value) {
    if (this[i].type == 'range') {
      switch (this[i].name) {
        // alpha_channel is between 0-1
        case 'alpha_channel': values.push(value / 100);
        ¬ break;
        // hue is a plain value from 0-360
        case 'hue': values.push(value); break;
        // default includes saturation & luminance as a
        ¬ percentage
        default: values.push(value + '%');
      }
    }
  }
  hsla.value = 'hsla(' + values.reverse().join(', ') + ')';
  preview.style.backgroundColor = hsla.value;
  rgba.value = getComputedStyle(preview, null).
  ¬ backgroundColor;
};
```

My final colour picker makes use of the range input type, the new onforminput event, and the new output elements to show the value (though this could easily use .innerHTML). The final result is shown in **Figure 3.13**.

FIGURE 3.13 An HSLA colour picker using the onforminput event.

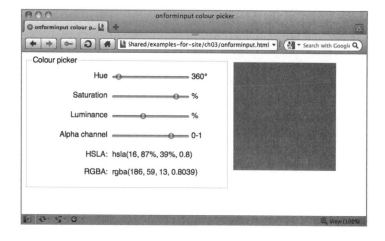

Summary

Hopefully you've seen that HTML5 forms offer a huge productivity boost for developers and a consistent user experience for users. They offer a ton of features right out of the box that previously would have required a lot of custom coding (such as form validation, or creating slider controls). Implementation is at varying, but increasing, levels in Opera, the WebKit browsers (Safari, Chrome), and beginning in Firefox. The lack of implementation in IE9 is fakable with JavaScript, as the new features are designed to degrade gracefully.

Now let's move on to even sexier subjects.

CHAPTER 4

Video and Audio

Bruce Lawson and Remy Sharp

A LONG TIME AGO, in a galaxy that feels a very long way away, multimedia on the Web was limited to tinkling MIDI tunes and animated GIFs. As bandwidth got faster and compression technologies improved, MP3 music supplanted MIDI and real video began to gain ground. All sorts of proprietary players battled it out—Real Player, Windows Media, and so on—until one emerged as the victor in 2005: Adobe Flash, largely because of the ubiquity of its plugin and the fact that it was the delivery mechanism of choice for YouTube.

HTML5 provides a competing, open standard for delivery of multimedia on the Web with its native video and audio elements and APIs. This chapter largely discusses the <video> element, as that's sexier, but most of the markup and scripting are applicable for both types of media.

Native multimedia: why, what, and how?

In 2007, Anne van Kesteren wrote to the Working Group:

"Opera has some internal experimental builds with an imple-mentation of a <video> element. The element exposes a simple API (for the moment) much like the Audio() object: play(), pause(), stop(). *The idea is that it works like* <object> *except that it has special* <video> *semantics much like* <img> *has image semantics."*

While the API has increased in complexity, van Kesteren's origi-nal announcement is now implemented in all the major brows-ers, and during the writing of this book Microsoft announced forthcoming support in Internet Explorer 9.

An obvious companion to a <video> element is an <audio> element; they share many similar features, so in this chapter we discuss them together and only note the differences.

<video>: Why do you need a <video> element?

Previously, if developers wanted to include video in a web page, they had to make use of the <object> element, which is a generic container for "foreign objects." Due to browser incon-sistencies, they would also need to use the previously invalid <embed> element and duplicate many parameters. This resulted in code that looked much like this:

```
<object width="425" height="344">
<param name="movie" value="http://www.youtube.com/
¬ v/9sEI1AUFJKw&hl=en_GB&fs=1&"></param>
<param name="allowFullScreen"
value="true"></param>
<param name="allowscriptaccess"
value="always"></param>
<embed src="http://www.youtube.com/
¬ v/9sEI1AUFJKw&hl=en_GB&fs=1&"
type="application/x-shockwave-flash"
allowscriptaccess="always"
allowfullscreen="true" width="425"
height="344"></embed>
</object>
```

This code is ugly and ungainly. Worse than that is the fact that the browser has to pass the video off to a third-party plugin; hope that the user has the correct version of that plugin (or has the rights to download and install it, or the knowledge of how to); and then hope that the plugin is keyboard accessible—along with all the other unknowns involved in handing the content to a third-party application.

Plugins can also be a significant cause of browser instability and can create worry in less technical users when they are prompted to download and install newer versions.

Whenever you include a plugin in your pages, you're reserving a certain drawing area that the browser delegates to the plugin. As far as the browser is concerned, the plugin's area remains a black box—the browser does not process or interpret anything that is happening there.

Normally, this is not a problem, but issues can arise when your layout overlaps the plugin's drawing area. Imagine, for example, a site that contains a movie but also has JavaScript or CSS-based dropdown menus that need to unfold over the movie. By default, the plugin's drawing area sits on top of the web page, meaning that these menus will strangely appear behind the movie.

Problems and quirks can also arise if your page has dynamic layout changes. If the dimensions of the plugin's drawing area are resized, this can sometimes have unforeseen effects—a movie playing in the plugin may not resize, but instead simply be cropped or display extra white space. HTML5 provides a standardised way to play video directly in the browser, with no plugins required.

> **NOTE** `<embed>` is finally standardised in HTML5; it was never part of any previous flavour of (X)HTML.

One of the major advantages of the HTML5 video element is that, finally, video is a full-fledged citizen on the Web. It's no longer shunted off to the hinterland of `<object>` or the non-validating `<embed>` element.

So now, `<video>` elements can be styled with CSS; they can be resized on hover using CSS transitions, for example. They can be tweaked and redisplayed onto `<canvas>` with JavaScript. Best of all, the innate hackability that open web standards provide is opened up. Previously, all your video data was locked away; your bits were trapped in a box. With HTML5 multimedia, your bits are free to be manipulated however you want.

What HTML5 multimedia isn't good for

Regardless of the somewhat black and white headlines of the tech journalists, HTML5 won't "kill" all plugins overnight. There are use-cases for plugins not covered by the new spec.

Copy protection is one area not dealt with by HTML5—unsurprisingly, given that it's a standard based on openness. So people who need DRM are probably not going to want to use HTML5 video or audio, as they will be as easy to download to a hard drive as an `<img>` is now. Some browsers offer simple context-menu access to the URL of the video, or even to save the video. (Of course, you don't need us to point out that DRM is a fools' errand, anyway. All you do is alienate your honest users while causing minor inconvenience to dedicated pirates.)

Plugins remain the best option for a browser to transmit video and audio from the user's machine to a web page such as Daily Mugshot or Chat Roulette. (There is a highly nascent `<device>` element rudimentarily specified for "post-5" HTML, but there is no support in browsers for it.) After shuddering at the unimaginable loneliness that a world without Chat Roulette would represent, consider also the massive amount of content out there that will require plugins to render it for a long time to come.

Anatomy of the video element

At its simplest, including video on a page in HTML5 merely requires this code:

```
<video src=turkish.ogv></video>
```

The .ogv file extension is used here to point to an Ogg Theora video.

> **NOTE** So long as the http end point is a streaming resource on the web, you can just point the `<video>` or `<audio>` element at it to stream the content.

Similar to `<object>`, you can put fallback markup between the tags, for older Web browsers that do not support native video. You should at least supply a link to the video so users can download it to their hard drives and watch it later on the operating system's media player. **Figure 4.1** shows this code in a modern browser and fallback content in a legacy browser.

```
<h1>Video and legacy browser fallback</h1>
<video src=leverage-a-synergy.ogv>
  Download the <a href=leverage-a-synergy.ogv>How to
  ¬ leverage a synergy video</a>
</video>
```

FIGURE 4.1 **HTML5** video in a modern browser and fallback content in a legacy browser.

However, this example won't actually do anything just yet. All you can see here is the first frame of the movie. That's because you haven't told the video to play, and you haven't told the browser to provide any controls for playing or pausing the video.

autoplay

You can tell the browser to play the video or audio automatically, but you almost certainly shouldn't, as many users (and particularly those using assistive technology, such as a screen reader) will find it highly intrusive. Users on mobile devices probably won't want you using their bandwidth without them explicitly asking for the video. Nevertheless, here's how you do it:

```
<video src=leverage-a-synergy.ogv autoplay>
</video>
```

controls

Providing controls is approximately 764 percent better than autoplaying your video. See **Figure 4.2**. You can use some simple JavaScript to write your own (more on that later) or you can tell the browser to provide them automatically:

```
<video src=leverage-a-synergy.ogv controls>
</video>
```

Naturally, these differ between browsers, in the same way that form controls do, for example, but you'll find nothing too surprising. There's a play/pause toggle, a seek bar, and volume control.

FIGURE 4.2 The default controls in Firefox 3.6 (similar in all modern browsers).

Notice that these controls appear when a user hovers over a video or when she tabs to the video. It's also possible to tab through the different controls. This native keyboard accessibility is already an improvement on plugins, which can be tricky to tab into from surrounding HTML content.

If the `<audio>` element has the controls attribute, you'll see them on the page. Without the attribute, nothing is rendered visually on the page at all, but is, of course, there in the DOM and fully controllable via JavaScript and the new APIs.

> **NOTE** Browsers have different levels of keyboard accessibility. Firefox's native controls don't appear when JavaScript is disabled (the contextual menu allows the user to stop and start the movie, but there is the issue of discoverability, and it doesn't seem possible to choose these options without JS.) Opera's accessible native controls are always present when JavaScript is disabled, regardless of whether the `controls` attribute is specified.
>
> Chrome and Safari have issues with keyboard accessibility. We anticipate increased keyboard accessibility as manufacturers iron out teething problems.

poster

The `poster` attribute points to an image that the browser will use while the video is downloading, or until the user tells the video to play. (This attribute is not applicable to `<audio>`.) It removes the need for additional tricks like displaying an image and then removing it via JavaScript when the video is started.

If you don't use the `poster` attribute, the browser shows the first frame of the movie, which may not be the representative image you want to show.

height, width

These attributes tell the browser the size in pixels of the video. (They are not applicable to `<audio>`.) If you leave them out, the browser uses the intrinsic width of the video resource, if that is available. Otherwise it is the intrinsic width of the poster frame, if that is available. Otherwise it is 300 pixels.

If you specify one value, but not the other, the browser adjusts the size of the unspecified dimension to preserve the video's aspect ratio.

If you set both width and height to an aspect ratio that doesn't match that of the video, the video is not stretched to those dimensions but is rendered "letter-boxed" inside the video element of your specified size while retaining the aspect ratio.

loop

The loop attribute is another Boolean attribute. As you would imagine, it loops the media playback.

preload

Maybe you're pretty sure that the user wants to activate the media (he's drilled down to it from some navigation, for example, or it's the only reason to be on the page), but you don't want to use autoplay. If so, you can suggest that the browser preload the video so that it begins buffering when the page loads in the expectation that the user will activate the controls.

```
<video src=leverage-a-synergy.ogv controls preload>
</video>
```

There are three spec-defined states of the preload attribute. If you just say preload, the user agent can decide what to do. A mobile browser may, for example, default to not preloading until explicitly told to do so by the user.

1. preload=auto (or just preload)

A suggestion to the browser that it should begin downloading the entire file. Note that we say "suggestion." The browser may ignore this—perhaps because it detected very slow connection or a setting in a mobile browser "Never preload media" to save the user's bandwidth.

2. preload=none

This state suggests to the browser that it shouldn't preload the resource until the user activates the controls.

3. preload=metadata

This state suggests to the browser that it should just prefetch metadata (dimensions, first frame, track list, duration, and so on) but that it shouldn't download anything further until the user activates the controls.

> **NOTE** The specification for preload changed in March 2010 and is not implemented anywhere as of April 2010.

src

As on an <img>, this attribute points to the file to be displayed. However, because not all browsers can play the same formats, in production environments you need to have more than one source file. We'll cover this in the next section. Using a single source file with the src attribute is only really useful for rapid prototyping or for intranet sites where you know the user's browser and which codecs it supports.

Codecs—the horror, the horror

Early drafts of the HTML5 specification mandated that all browsers should at least have built-in support for multimedia in two codecs: Ogg Vorbis for audio and Ogg Theora for movies. Vorbis is a codec used by services like Spotify, among others, and for audio samples in games like Microsoft Halo, it's often used with Theora for video and combined together in the Ogg container format.

However, these codecs were dropped from the HTML5 spec after Apple and Nokia objected, so the spec makes no recommendations about codecs at all. This leaves us with a fragmented situation. Opera and Firefox support Theora and Vorbis. Safari doesn't, preferring instead to provide native support for the H.264 video codec and MP3 audio. Microsoft has announced that IE9 will also support H.264, which is also supported on iPhone and Android. Google Chrome supports Theora and H.264 video, and Vorbis and MP3 audio. Confused?

As we were finishing this book, Google announced it is open-sourcing a video codec called VP8. This is a very high-quality codec, and when combined with Vorbis in a container format based on the Matroska format, it's collectively known as "webM".

Opera, Firefox and Chrome have announced it will support it. IE9 will, if the codec is separately installed. VP8 will be included in Adobe's Flash Player and every YouTube video will be in webM format.

Like Theora, it's a royalty-free codec. In this chapter, you can substitute .ogv examples with .webm for high quality video, once browser support is there.

The rule is: provide both royalty-free (webM or Theora) *and* H.264 video in your pages, and both Vorbis and MP3 audio so that nobody gets locked out of your content. Let's not repeat the mistakes of the old "Best viewed in Netscape Navigator" badges on websites.

Multiple <source> elements

To do this, you need to encode your multimedia twice: once as Theora and once as H.264 in the case of video, and in both Vorbis and MP3 for audio.

Then, you tie these separate versions of the file to the media element. Instead of using the single src attribute, you nest separate <source> elements for each encoding with appropriate type attributes inside the <audio> or <video> element and let the browser download the format that it can display.

Note that in this case we do not provide a src attribute in the media element itself:

```
1   <video controls>
2       <source src=leverage-a-synergy.ogv type='video/ogg;
        ¬codecs="theora, vorbis"'>
3       <source src=leverage-a-synergy.mp4 type='video/mp4;
        ¬codecs="avc1.42E01E, mp4a.40.2"'>
4   <p>Your browser doesn't support video.
5   Please download the video in <a href=leverage-a-
    ¬synergy.ogv>Ogg</a> or <a href=leverage-a-
    ¬synergy.mp4>mp4</a> format.</p>
6   </video>
```

NOTE Stop press: iPad bug: Since going to press we've been told of a bug that affects some iPads that means they can only read the first <source> element. Therefore your mp4 version should come before your royalty-free version in the source order.

Line 1 tells the browser that a video is to be inserted and to give it default controls. Line 2 offers an Ogg Theora video and uses the type attribute to tell the browser what kind of container format is used (by giving the file's MIME type) and what codec was used for the encoding of the video and the audio stream. We could also offer a WebM video here as a high-quality royalty-free option. Notice that we used quotation marks around these parameters. If you miss out on the type attribute, the browser downloads a small bit of each file before it figures out that it is unsupported, which wastes bandwidth and could delay the media playing.

Line 3 offers an H.264 video. The codec strings for H.264 and AAC are more complicated than those for Ogg because there are several profiles for H.264 and AAC. Higher profiles require more CPU to decode, but they are better compressed and take less bandwidth.

Inside the <video> element is our fallback message, including links to *both* formats for browsers that can natively deal with neither video type but which is probably on top of an operating system that can deal with one of the formats, so the user can download the file and watch it in a media player outside the browser.

OK, so that's native HTML5 video for all users of modern browsers. What about users of legacy browsers—including Internet Explorer 8 and older?

Video for legacy browsers

Older browsers can't play native video or audio, bless them. But if you're prepared to rely on plugins, you can ensure that users of older browsers can still experience your content in a way that is no worse than they currently get.

> **NOTE** The content between the tags is fallback content only for browsers that do not support the <video> element at all. A browser that understands HTML5 video but can't play any of the formats that your code points to will not display the "fallback" content between the tags. This has bitten me on the bottom a few times. Sadly, there is no video record of that.

Remember that the contents of the <video> element can contain markup, like the text and links in the previous example? Because the MP4 file type can also be played by the Flash player plugin, you can use the MP4 movie in combination as a fallback for Internet Explorer 8 and older versions of other browsers.

The code for this is as hideous as you'd expect for a transitional hack, but it works everywhere a Flash Player is installed—which is almost everywhere. You can see this nifty technique in an article called "Video for Everybody!" by its inventor, Kroc Camen **http://camendesign.com/code/video_for_everybody**.

Alternatively, you could host the fallback content on a video hosting site and embed a link to that between the tags of a video element:

```
<video controls>
    <source src=leverage-a-synergy.ogv type='video/ogg;
    ¬ codecs="theora, vorbis"'>
    <source src=leverage-a-synergy.mp4 type='video/mp4;
    ¬ codecs="avc1.42E01E, mp4a.40.2"'>
<embed src="http://www.youtube.com/v/cmtcc94Tv3A&hl=
¬ en_GB&fs=1&rel=0" type="application/x-shockwave-flash"
```

```
¬allowscriptaccess="always" allowfullscreen="true"
¬width="425" height="344">
</video>
```

You can use the html5media library **http://static.etianen.com/ html5media/** to hijack the <video> element and automagically add necessary fallback by adding one line of JavaScript in the head of your page.

Encoding royalty-free video and audio

Ideally, you should start the conversion from the source format itself, rather than recompressing an already compressed version. Double compression can seriously reduce the quality of the final output.

On the audio side of things, the open-source audio editing software Audacity (**http://audacity.sourceforge. net/**) has built-in support for Ogg Vorbis export. For video conversion, there are a few good choices. For .WebM, there are only a few encoders at the moment, unsurprisingly for such a new codec. See **www.webmproject.org/tools/** for the growing list.

The free application evom (**http://thelittleappfactory.com/evom/**) can make Ogg Theora on a Mac through a nice graphical interface. Windows and Mac users can download Miro Video Converter (**www.mirovideoconverter.com/**), which allows you to drag a file into its window for conversion into Theora or H.264 optimised for different devices such as iPhone, Android Nexus One, PS2, and so on.

The free VLC (**www.videolan.org/vlc/**) can convert files to Ogg on Windows or Linux. OggConvert (**http://oggconvert.tristanb.net/**) is a useful utility for Linux users.

Alternatively, the Firefox extension Firefogg and its associated website **http://firefogg.org/** provides an easy web-based conversion. TinyOgg (**http://tinyogg.com/**) converts Flash video to Ogg for download, and can even be fed a YouTube URL.

The conversion process can also be automated and handled server-side. For instance in a CMS environment, you may not be able to control the format in which authors upload their files, so you may want to do compression at the server end. The open-source ffmpeg library (**http://ffmpeg.org/**) can be installed on a server to bring industrial-strength conversions of uploaded files (maybe you're starting your own YouTube-killer?)

If you're worried about storage space and you're happy to share your media files (audio and video) under one of the various CC licenses, have a look at the Internet Archive (**www.archive.org/create/**) which will convert and host them for you. Just create a password and upload, then use a <video> element on your page but link to the source file on their servers.

Sending differently-compressed videos to handheld devices

Video files tend to be large, and sending very high-quality video can be wasteful if sent to handheld devices where the small screen sizes make high quality unnecessary. There's no point in sending high-definition video meant for a widescreen monitor to a handheld device screen. Compressing a video down to a size appropriate for a small screen can save a lot of bandwidth, making your server and—most importantly—your mobile users happy.

HTML5 allows you to use the `media` attribute on the source element, which queries the browser to find out screen size (or number of colours, aspect ratio, and so on) and send different files that are optimised for different screen sizes.

> **NOTE** We use `min-device-width` rather than `min-width` to cater to devices that have a viewport into the content—that is, every full-featured smartphone browser, as this gives us the width of the viewport display.

This functionality and syntax is borrowed from the CSS Media Queries specification **dev.w3.org/csswg/css3-mediaqueries/**) but is part of the markup, as we're switching source files depending on device characteristics. In the following example, the browser is "asked" if it has a min-device-width of 800px—that is, does it have a wide screen. If it does, it receives `hi-res.ogv`; if not, it is sent `lo-res.ogv`:

```
<video controls>
        <source src=hi-res.ogv ... media="(min-device-width:
        ¬ 800px)">
        <source src=lo-res.ogv>
</video>
```

Also note that you should still use the type attribute with codecs parameters and fallback content previously discussed. We've just omitted those for clarity.

Rolling custom controls

One truly spiffing aspect of the media element, and therefore the audio and video elements, is that the JavaScript API is super easy. The API for both audio and video descend from the same media API, so they're nearly exactly the same. The only difference in these elements is that the video element has `height` and `width` attributes and a `poster` attribute. The events, the methods, and all other attributes are the same. With that in mind, we'll stick with the sexier media element: the `<video>` element for our JavaScript discussion.

As you saw at the start of this chapter, Anne van Kesteren talks about the new API and that we have new simple methods such as `play()`, `pause()` (there's no stop method: simply pause and and move to the start), `load()`, and `canPlayType()`. In fact, that's *all* the methods on the media element. Everything else is events and attributes.

Table 4.1 provides a reference list of media attributes and events.

TABLE 4.1 **Media Attributes and Events**

ATTRIBUTES	METHODS
error state	load()
error	canPlayType(type)
network state	play()
src	pause()
currentSrc	addTrack(label, kind, language)
networkState	
preload	events
buffered	loadstart
ready state	progress
readyState	suspend
seeking	abort
controls	error
controls	emptied
volume	stalled
muted	play
tracks	pause
tracks	loadedmetadata
playback state	loadeddata
currentTime	waiting
startTime	playing
duration	canplay
paused	canplaythrough
defaultPlaybackRate	seeking
playbackRate	seeked
played	timeupdate
seekable	ended
ended	ratechange
autoplay	
loop	
video specific	
width	
height	
videoWidth	
videoHeight	
poster	

Using JavaScript and the new media API you can create and manage your own video player controls. In our example, we walk you through some of the ways to control the video element and create a simple set of controls. Our example won't blow your mind—it isn't nearly as sexy as the video element itself (and is a little contrived!)—but you'll get a good idea of what's possible through scripting. The best bit is that the UI will be all CSS and HTML. So if you want to style it your own way, it's easy with just a bit of web standards knowledge—no need to edit an external Flash player or similar.

Our hand-rolled basic video player controls will have a play/pause toggle button and allow the user to scrub along the timeline of the video to skip to a specific section, as shown in **Figure 4.3**.

FIGURE 4.3 Our simple but custom video player controls.

Our starting point will be a video with native controls enabled. We'll then use JavaScript to strip the native controls and add our own, so that if JavaScript is disabled, the user still has a way to control the video as we intended:

```
<video controls>
    <source src="leverage-a-synergy.ogv" type="video/ogg" />
    <source src="leverage-a-synergy.mp4" type="video/mp4" />
    Your browser doesn't support video.
    Please download the video in <a href="leverage-a-
    ¬ synergy.ogv">Ogg</a> or <a href="leverage-a-
    ¬ synergy.mp4">MP4</a> format.
</video>
<script>
var video = document.getElementsByTagName('video')[0];
video.removeAttribute('controls');
</script>
```

Play, pause, and toggling playback

Next, we want to be able to play and pause the video from a custom control. We've included a button element that we're going to bind a click handler and do the play/pause functionality from. Throughout my code examples, when I refer to the play variable it will refer to the button element:

```
<button class="play" title="play">&#x25BA;</button/>
```

We're using ►, which is a geometric XML entity that *looks* like a play button. Once the button is clicked, we'll start the video and switch the value to two pipes using ▐, which looks (a little) like a pause, as shown in **Figure 4.4**.

▶ ►

▌▌ ▐ (twice)

FIGURE 4.4 **Using XML** entities to represent play and pause buttons.

For simplicity, I've included the button element as markup, but as we're progressively enhancing our video controls, all of these additional elements (for play, pause, scrubbing, and so on) should be generated by the JavaScript.

In the play/pause toggle we have a number of things to do:

1. If the video is currently paused, start playing, or if the video has finished then we need to reset the current time to 0, that is, move the playhead back to the start of the video.

2. Change the toggle button's value to show that the next time the user clicks, it will toggle from pause to play or play to pause.

3. Finally, we play (or pause) the video:

```
if (video.paused || video.ended) {
  if (video.ended) {
    video.currentTime = 0;
  }
  this.innerHTML = '▌▌'; // &#x2590;&#x2590; doesn't need
  ¬ escaping here
  this.title = 'pause';
  video.play();
} else {
  this.innerHTML = '▶'; // &#x25BA;
  this.title = 'play';
  video.pause();
}
```

The problem with this logic is that we're relying entirely on our own script to determine the state of the play/pause button. What if the user was able to pause or play the video via the native video element controls somehow (some browsers allow the user to right click and select to play and pause the video)? Also, when the video comes to the end, the play/pause button would still show a pause icon. Ultimately we need our controls to always relate to the state of the video.

Eventful media elements

The media elements fire a broad range of events: when playback starts, when a video has finished loading, if the volume has changed, and so on. So, getting back to our custom play/pause button, we strip the part of the script that deals with changing its visible label:

```
if (video.ended) {
  video.currentTime = 0;
}
if (video.paused) {
  video.play();
} else {
  video.pause();
}
// which could be written as: video[video.paused ? 'play' :
¬ 'pause']();
```

> **NOTE** In these examples we're using the addEventListener DOM level 2 API, rather than the attachEvent, which is specific to Internet Explorer up to version 8. The upcoming IE9 will support video, but it thankfully also supports the standardised addEventListener, so our code will work there, too.

In the simplified code if the video has ended, we reset it, then toggle the playback based on its current state. The label on the control itself is updated by separate (anonymous) functions we've hooked straight into the event handlers on our video element:

```
video.addEventListener('play', function () {
  play.title = 'pause';
  play.innerHTML = '❚❚';
}, false);
video.addEventListener('pause', function () {
  play.title = 'play';
  play.innerHTML = '▶';
}, false);
video.addEventListener('ended', function () {
  this.pause();
}, false);
```

Now whenever the video is played, paused, or has reached the end, the function associated with the relevant event is fired, making sure that our control shows the right label.

Now that we're handling playing and pausing, we want to show the user how much of the video has downloaded and therefore how much is playable. This would be the amount of *buffered* video available. We also want to catch the event that says how much video has been played, so we can move our visual slider to the appropriate location to show how far through the video we are, as shown in **Figure 4.5**. Finally, and most importantly, we need to capture the event that says the video is *ready* to be played, that is, there's enough video data to start watching.

FIGURE 4.5 **Our custom video progress bar, including seekable content and the current playhead position.**

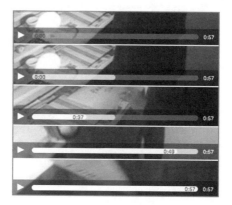

Monitoring download progress

The media element has a "progress" event, which fires once the media has been fetched but potentially before the media has been processed. When this event fires, we can read the `video. seekable` object, which has a `length`, `start()`, and `end()` method. We can update our seek bar (shown in Figure 4.5 in the second frame with the whiter colour) using the following code (where the buffer variable is the element that shows how much of the video we can seek and has been downloaded):

```
video.addEventListener('progress', updateSeekable, false);
function updateSeekable() {
  var endVal = this.seekable && this.seekable.length ?
  ¬ this.seekable.end() : 0;
  buffer.style.width = (100 / (this.duration || 1) *
  ¬ endVal) + '%';
}
```

The code binds to the progress event, and when it fires, it gets the percentage of video that can be played back compared to the length of the video. Note that the keyword this refers to the video element, as that's the context in which the updateSeekable function will be executed, and the duration attribute is the length of the media in seconds

However, there's sometimes a subtle issue in Firefox in its video element that causes the video.seekable.end() value *not* to be the same as the duration. Or rather, once the media is fully downloaded and processed, the final duration doesn't match the video.seekable.end() value. To work around this issue, we can also listen for the durationchange event using the same updateSeekable function. This way, if the duration does change *after* the last process event, the durationchange event fires and our buffer element will have the correct width:

```
video.addEventListener('durationchange', updateSeekable,
¬ false);
video.addEventListener('progress', updateSeekable, false);
function updateSeekable() {
   buffer.style.width = (100 / (this.duration || 1) *
      (this.seekable && this.seekable.length ? this.seekable.
      ¬ end() : 0)) + '%';
}
```

When the media file is ready to play

When your browser first encounters the video (or audio) element on a page, the media file isn't ready to be played just yet. The browser needs to download and then decode the video (or audio) so it can be played. Once that's complete, the media element will fire the canplay event. *Typically* this is the time you would initialise your controls and remove any "loading" indicator. So our code to initialise the controls would *typically* look like this:

```
video.addEventListener('canplay', initialiseControls,
¬ false);
```

Nothing terribly exciting there. The control initialisation enables the play/pause toggle button and resets the playhead in the seek bar.

> **NOTE** The events to do with loading fire in the following order: loadstart, durationchange, loadeddata, progress, canplay, canplaythrough.

However, sometimes this event won't fire right away (or at least when you're expecting it to fire). Sometimes the video suspends download because the browser is trying to save downloading too much for you. That can be a headache if you're expecting the canplay event, which won't fire unless you give the media element a bit of a kicking. So instead, we've started listening for the loadeddata event. This says that there's some data that's been loaded, though not particularly all the data. This means that the metadata is available (height, width, duration, and so on) and *some* media content—but not *all* of it. By allowing the user to start to play the video at the point in which loadeddata has fired, it forces browsers like Firefox to go from a suspended state to downloading the rest of the media content, allowing it to play the whole video. So, in fact, the correct point in the event cycle to enable the user interface is the loadeddata:

```
video.addEventListener('loadeddata', initialiseControls,
¬false);
```

Preloading metadata

A recent addition to the media element is the preload attribute (so new that it's not supported in browsers right now). It allows developers to tell browsers only to download the header information about the media element, which would include the metadata. If support for this attribute does make its way into browsers, it stands to reason we should listen for the loadedmetadata event over the loadeddata event if you wanted to initalise the duration and slider controls of the media.

Fast forward, slow motion, and reverse

The spec provides an attribute, playbackRate. By default the assumed playbackRate is 1, meaning normal playback at the intrinsic speed of the media file. Increasing this attribute speeds up the playback; decreasing it slows it down. Negative values indicate that the video will play in reverse.

Not all browsers support playbackRate yet (only WebKit-based browsers support it right now), so if you need to support fast forward and rewind, you can hack around this by programmatically changing currentTime:

```
function speedup(video, direction) {
  if (direction == undefined) direction = 1; // or -1 for
  ¬reverse

  if (video.playbackRate != undefined) {
    video.playbackRate = direction == 1 ? 2 : -2;
  } else { // do it manually
```

```
    video.setAttribute('data-playbackRate', setInterval
    ¬((function playbackRate () {
      video.currentTime += direction;
      return playbackRate; // allows us to run the
      ¬function once and setInterval
    })(), 500));
  }
}

function playnormal(video) {
  if (video.playbackRate != undefined) {
    video.playbackRate = 1;
  } else { // do it manually
    clearInterval(video.getAttribute('data-playbackRate'));
  }
}
```

As you can see from the previous example, if playbackRate is supported, you can set positive and negative numbers to control the direction of playback. In addition to being able to rewind and fast forward using the playbackRate, you can also use a fraction to play the media back in slow motion using video.playbackRate = 0.5, which plays at half the normal rate.

Multimedia accessibility

We've talked about the keyboard accessibility of the video element, but what about transcripts, captions for multimedia? After all, there is no alt attribute for video or audio as there is for <img>. The fallback content between the tags is only meant for browsers that can't cope with native video; not for people whose browsers can display the media but can't see or hear it due to disability or situation (for example, in a noisy environment or needing to conserve bandwidth).

The theory of HTML5 multimedia accessibility is excellent. The original author should make a subtitle file and put it in the container Ogg or MP4 file along with the multimedia files, and the browser will offer a user interface whereby the user can get those captions or subtitles. Even if the video is "embedded" on 1,000 different sites (simply by using an external URL as the source of the video/audio element), those sites get the subtitling information for free, so we get "write once, read everywhere" accessibility.

That's the theory. In practice, no one knows how to do this; the spec is silent, browsers do nothing. That's starting to change; at the time of this writing (May 2010), the WHATWG have added a new ‹track› element to the spec, which allows addition of various kinds of information such as subtitles, captions, description, chapter titles, and metadata.

The WHATWG is specifying a new timed text format called WebSRT (**www.whatwg.org/specs/web-apps/current-work/ multipage/video.html#websrt**) for this information, which is one reason that this shadowy 29th element isn't in the W3C version of the spec. The format of the ‹track› element is

```
<track kind=captions src=captions.srt>
```

But what can you do right now? There is no one true approach to this problem, but here we'll present one possible (albeit hacky) interim solution.

Bruce made a proof of concept that displays individual lines of a transcript, which have been timestamped using the new HTML5 data-* attributes:

```
<article class=transcript lang=en>
<p><span data-begin=3 data-end=5>Hello, good evening and
¬welcome.</span>
<span data-begin=7.35 data-end=9.25>Let's welcome Mr Last
¬Week, singing his poptabulous hit &ldquot;If I could turn
¬back time!&rdquot;</span>
</p>
...
</article>
```

JavaScript is used to hide the transcript ‹article›, hook into the timeupdate event of the video API, and overlay spans as plain text (therefore stylable with CSS) over (or next to) the video element, depending on the current playback time of the video and the timestamps on the individual spans. See it in action at **http:// dev.opera.com/articles/view/accessible-html5-video-with-javas-cripted-captions/**. See **Figure 4.6**.

FIGURE 4.6 The script superimposes the caption over the video as delectable selectable text.

The data-* attributes (custom data attributes)

HTML5 allows custom attributes on any element. These can be used to pass information to local scripts.

Previously, to store custom data in your markup, authors would do something annoying like use classes: `<input class="spaceship shields-5 lives-3 energy-75">`. Then your script would need to waste time grabbing these class names, such as `shields-5`, splitting them at a delimiter (a hyphen in this example) to extract the value. In his book, *PPK on JavaScript* (New Riders, ISBN 0321423305), Peter Paul Koch explains how to do this and why he elected to use custom attributes in some HTML4 pages, making the JavaScript leaner and easier to write but also making the page technically invalid. As it's much easier to use `data-shields=5` for passing name/value pairs to scripts, HTML5 legitimises and standardises this useful, real-world practice.

We're using `data-begin` and `data-end`; they could just as legitimately be `data-start` and `data-finish`, or (in a different genre of video) `data-ooh-matron` and `data-slapandtickle`. Like choosing class or id names, you should pick a name that matches the semantics.

Custom data attributes are only meant for passing information to the site's own scripts, for which there are no more appropriate attributes or elements.

The spec says "These attributes are not intended for use by software that is independent of the site that uses the attributes" and are therefore not intended to pass information to crawlers or third-party parsers. That's a job for microformats, microdata, or RDFa.

When the `data-*` attributes are fully supported in a browser, JavaScript can access the properties using `element.dataset.foo` (where the `data-foo` attribute contains the value). Support can be emulated using JavaScript by extending the `HTMLElement` object, which typically isn't possible in IE9 alpha release and below, which you can see here: **http://gist.github.com/362081**. Otherwise scripts can access the values via the `get/setAttribute` methods. The advantage of the dataset property over `setAttribute` is that it can be enumerated, but also, when fully implemented in browsers, setting a dataset attribute automatically sets the content attribute on the element giving you a shorthand syntax for setting custom data.

For more information, see the spec **http://dev.w3.org/html5/spec/Overview.html#custom-data-attribute**.

The BBC has a similar experiment at **http://open.bbc.co.uk/ rad/demos/html5/rdtv/episode2/** that takes in subtitles from an external JavaScript file **http://open.bbc.co.uk/rad/demos/html5/ rdtv/episode2/rdtv-episode2.js**, which is closer to the vision of HTML5, but it doesn't have the side effect of allowing search engines to index the contents of the transcript.

Silvia Pfeiffer, a contractor for Mozilla, has some clever demos using HTML5 videos and some extra extensions (that are not part of the spec) at **www.annodex.net/~silvia/itext/**.

Summary

You've seen how HTML5 gives you the first credible alternative to third-party plugins. The incompatible codec support currently makes it harder than using plugins to simply embed video in a page and have it work cross-browser.

On the plus side, because video and audio are now regular elements natively supported by the browser (rather than a "black box" plugin) and offer a powerful API, they're extremely easy to control via JavaScript. With nothing more than a bit of web standards knowledge, developers can easily build their own custom controls, or do all sorts of crazy video manipulation with only a few lines of code. As a safety net for browsers that can't cope, we recommend that you also add links to download your video files outside the `<video>` element.

There are already a number of ready-made scripts available that allow you to easily leverage the HTML5 synergies in your own pages, without having to do all the coding yourself. The Kaltura player (**http://www.html5video.org/**) is an open source video player that works in all browsers. jPlayer (**http://www.happyworm. com/jquery/jplayer/**) is a very liberally-licensed jQuery audio player that degrades to Flash in legacy browsers, can be styled with CSS and can be extended to allow playlists.

Accessing video with JavaScript is more than writing new players. In the next chapter, you'll learn how to manipulate native media elements for some truly amazing effects. Or at least, our heads bouncing around the screen—and who could conceive of anything amazinger than that?

CHAPTER 5

Canvas

Remy Sharp

IF THE VIDEO element is the poster boy of HTML5, the canvas element is definitely the Han Solo of HTML5. It's one of the larger parts of the HTML5 specification, and in fact the canvas API, the *2D drawing context*, has been split into a separate document, though the canvas element itself *is* still part of the official HTML5 spec.

The canvas element provides an API for 2D drawing— lines, fills, images, text, and so on. If you think back to the days of the version of MS Paint that came with Windows 95, you can imagine some of the functionality. In fact, Paint has been replicated using the canvas element, as shown in **Figure 5.1**. Drawing applications that aim to become fully fledged vector drawing applications are starting to pop up all over the web (**Figure 5.2**). As these applications are based on Open Web technology, they work in a browser on more devices, too. The Harmony application shown in **Figure 5.3** even works on mobile devices, including the iPhone and Android phones.

FIGURE 5.1 MS Paint replicated using the canvas element.

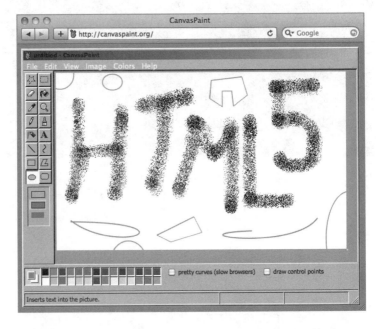

FIGURE 5.2 More-advanced drawing applications are emerging using canvas.

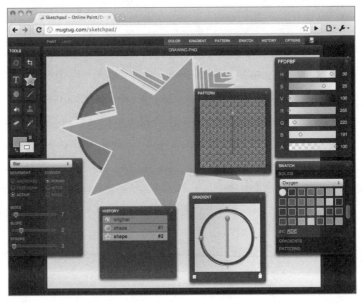

FIGURE 5.3 The canvas drawing demo Harmony also works, unmodified, on mobile browsers.

The API has already been used for a huge range of applications, including (interactive) backgrounds to websites, navigation elements, graphing tools, fully fledged applications, and games and emulators. Who knew Super Mario canvas–based games would open the eyes of so many developers!

The 2D API is large enough that I suspect we'll see entire books dedicated to the subject. Since I have only one chapter to talk about it, I'll show you the basics. But I'll also show you some of the funky stuff you can do with the canvas element, like capturing frames from a video or processing individual pixels from an image inside the canvas. I'll even show you how to export to files ready to be saved to your desktop. I'll also show you how to create your first animation, which might even hark back to the days of BASIC computing.

Canvas basics

> **NOTE** `querySelector` and `querySelectorAll` is a new DOM API that accepts a CSS selector and returns the elements it matches. Currently available in all the latest browsers, `querySelector` returns the first DOM node it finds, whereas `querySelectorAll` returns a `NodeList` object that you'll need to iterate over.

FIGURE 5.4 A filled rectangle using the default settings on a canvas.

The `hello world` of any canvas demo starts with putting the canvas element on your page. Initially the canvas is completely invisible and by default is 300 pixels wide by 150 pixels high:

```
<!DOCTYPE html>
<title>canvas hello world</title>
<canvas></canvas>
```

Now that the canvas element is in place, you need to use JavaScript to get the 2D context to allow you to draw:

```
var ctx = document.querySelector('canvas').getContext('2d');
```

Now that you have the context, you have access to the full API to draw as you please. Add simple shapes to your canvas (**Figure 5.4**):

```
ctx.fillRect(10, 20, 50, 50);
```

What about browser support?

Browser support is fairly good for the canvas element; four of the big five browsers support canvas in the latest versions of the browser (and in fact support is fairly good in previous versions of the browsers, too). "What about IE?" is the question that is perpetually asked.

For versions of IE that don't support canvas, you can shim canvas support in a couple of ways. The first is via Silverlight and a library called html5canvas (**http://blogs.msdn.com/delay/archive/2009/08/24/using-one-platform-to-build-another-html-5-s-canvas-tag-implemented-using-silverlight.aspx**); the second is using excanvas (**http://code.google.com/p/explorercanvas/**), which translates the canvas API to Microsoft's VML.

The two libraries don't cover *all* of the 2D API, but most of the commonly used methods. Several demos show comparisons from examples in the wild. Theoretically, you *could* try mixing the shims together; if Silverlight isn't available, drop support down to excanvas. I've not yet seen this done in practice, but in theory I can't see any reason why it wouldn't work, so long as you can detect Silverlight support.

FIGURE 5.5 Using fill styles and rectangle strokes.

* **TIP** The entire coordinates system in the 2D drawing API works in the same way CSS coordinates work, in that you work from the top-left to the bottom-right.

The arguments to `fillRect` are x, y, width, and height. The x and y coordinates start in the top left. As shown in Figure 5.4, the default colour is black. Add some colour and also draw an outline around the canvas so that the canvas looks like **Figure 5.5**:

```
ctx.fillStyle = 'rgb(0, 255, 0)';
ctx.fillRect(10, 20, 50, 50); // creates a solid square
ctx.strokeStyle = 'rgb(0, 182, 0)';
ctx.lineWidth = 5;
ctx.strokeRect(9, 19, 52, 52); // draws an outline
```

In the previous code listing, you're drawing twice on the canvas: once with `fillRect` and once with `strokeRect`. When you're not drawing, you're setting the colour and style of the 2D context which must happen before the fill or stroke happens, otherwise the default colour of black is used. Along with CSS colours being used in the `fillStyle` and `strokeStyle` (for example, RGB, hex, RGBA, and so on), you can also use gradients and patterns generated using the 2D API.

Painting gradients and patterns

Using the context object, you can generate a fill style that can be a linear gradient, radial gradient, or a pattern fill, which in turn can be used as the `fillStyle` on the canvas. Gradients and radial gradients work similar to CSS gradients (currently available in WebKit and Firefox 3.6), in that you specify a start point and colour stops for the gradient.

Patterns, on the other hand, allow you to point to an image source and then specify how the pattern should repeat, again similar to the repeat process on a CSS background image. What makes `createPattern` really interesting is that the image source can be an image, another canvas, or a video element (though at time of writing, using video as a source isn't implemented yet).

Creating a simple gradient is easy and possibly even faster than starting up Photoshop:

```
var canvas = document.querySelector('canvas'),
    ctx = canvas.getContext('2d'),
    gradient = ctx.createLinearGradient(0, 0, 0, canvas.
    ¬height);
gradient.addColorStop(0, '#fff');
gradient.addColorStop(1, '#000');
ctx.fillStyle = gradient;
ctx.fillRect(0, 0, canvas.width, canvas.height);
```

FIGURE 5.6 A vertical gradient on a canvas element.

The code in the previous listing uses the 2D context object to generate a linear gradient object to which you can then apply colour stops. The arguments are the starting point of the gradient, x1 and y1, and the end point of the gradient, x2 and y2. In this example, I'm telling the gradient to start in the top left and finish at the bottom of the canvas on the left. This creates a gradient that runs vertically (**Figure 5.6**).

Radial gradients are very similar, except the createRadialGradient takes the radius after each coordinate:

```
var canvas = document.querySelector('canvas'),
    ctx = canvas.getContext('2d'),
    gradient = ctx.createRadialGradient(canvas.width/2,
      canvas.height/2, 0,
      canvas.width/2, canvas.height/2, 150);
gradient.addColorStop(0, '#fff');
gradient.addColorStop(1, '#000');
ctx.fillStyle = gradient;
ctx.fillRect(0, 0, canvas.width, canvas.width);
```

FIGURE 5.7 A radial gradient that starts and ends from the same point, but the ending radius is much greater causing a smooth circular gradient.

The only difference is what kind of gradient you've created. In this example, I've moved the first point of the gradient to start in the centre of the canvas starting with a radius of zero. The gradient uses a radius of 150 radians, but notice that it also starts in the same place: canvas.width/2, canvas.height/2. This is so my example creates a nice smooth circular gradient (**Figure 5.7**).

Getting from degrees to radians

All the radius and arc methods use radians, so if you're used to working with degrees, you'll need to convert them to radians. Here's the JavaScript you need to go from degrees to radians:

```
var radians = degrees * Math.PI / 180;
```

It's also common to pass 360 degrees to the drawing methods, which is simply Math.PI * 2, and equally 180 degrees is Math.PI.

Patterns are even easier to use. You need a source, then you can drop the source element into the createPattern method and use the result as the fillStyle. The only caveat is that the element must have finished loading, in the case of images and videos, to capture the source properly.

To create the effect shown in **Figure 5.8** (a tiled image across the back of the canvas), stretch the canvas over the size of the window. Then dynamically create an image and when it fires the load event, use the image as the source of a repeating pattern:

```
var canvas = document.querySelector('canvas'),
    img = document.createElement('img'),
    ctx = canvas.getContext('2d');
canvas.width = window.innerWidth;
canvas.height = window.innerHeight;
img.onload = function () {
  ctx.fillStyle = ctx.createPattern(this, 'repeat');
  ctx.fillRect(0, 0, canvas.width, canvas.height);
};
img.src = 'remysharp_avatar.jpg';
```

FIGURE 5.8 Tilling an image on a canvas using the createPattern method.

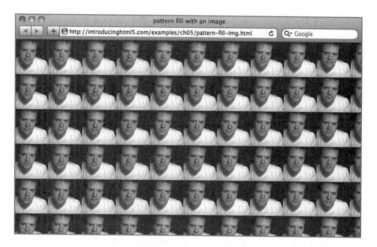

In this example I've created an image on the fly using document.createElement, only once the onload event fires do I continue to and build the pattern fill. You need to wait until all the data has loaded in to the image before you can begin to use it.

Now that the image is loaded, I'm able to set the fillStyle using createPattern. I've used createPattern(this, 'repeat'), and this refers to the image that fired the load event, but I can just as easily use another canvas as the source. The string 'repeat' follows the same syntax as CSS background-repeat, in that repeat-x, repeat-y, and no-repeat also work.

Keep in mind that when you resize a stretched canvas (as the example has), the contents of the canvas get stretched, just like Flash would do if it was resized (**Figure 5.9**). This is the same result as Figure 5.8 but I have resized the browser window after the drawing has completed.

FIGURE 5.9 When a canvas stretches after it's finished drawing, so does the contents of the canvas.

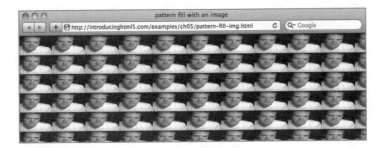

Drawing paths

FIGURE 5.10 My contrived stick man drawing using the path API.

Within the 2D API is a path API that allows you to move around the canvas and draw lines or shapes. The contrived example in **Figure 5.10** shows a stick man drawn using the path API.

I won't take you through all the code used to produce the stick man, just the highlights so you can see what methods I used. To draw the stick man, you must specify the x, y coordinates around the canvas that you want to draw, painstakingly specifying each individual line. To draw the stick man head, run the following code:

```
ctx.beginPath();
ctx.arc(100, 50, 30, 0, Math.PI*2, true); // head
ctx.fill();
```

This gives you a solid, filled head. I've given the x, y coordinates of 100, 50, respectively, and a radius of 30 pixels. The next arguments are the start and end points in radians. In this example, I want a complete circle, so I start at zero and end at Math.PI*2, which is equal to 360 degrees. Finally the sixth argument is the direction to draw the arc: clockwise or counter-clockwise. In this case it doesn't matter, but it's still required.

Once the head is drawn, I want to draw a face. The smile and eyes will be in red. When I draw the facial features, I need to use beginPath again. **Figure 5.11** shows you the result if I

FIGURE 5.11 An example of how a continued path causes an error in the final drawing.

didn't use beginPath. This is because the previous arc line I drew would be included in the final face path, but also because I'm starting a new arc for the mouth, as you'll see in the following code listing. I could fix the line joining the edge of the head to the mouth by using moveTo, which is effectively *lifting the pen* from the canvas to begin drawing someplace else, but I don't want the coloured outline around the head.

```
ctx.beginPath();
// draw the smile
ctx.strokeStyle = '#c00';
ctx.lineWidth = 3;
ctx.arc(100, 50, 20, 0, Math.PI, false);
ctx.stroke();
```

The previous code listing gives me a nice semi-circle for the smile with a new stroke colour and width. For the head I used fill, but for the face I need to use stroke, which will draw the line rather than a solid shape. Next the eyes:

```
ctx.beginPath();
ctx.fillStyle = '#c00';
// start the left eye
ctx.arc(90, 45, 3, 0, Math.PI*2, true);
ctx.fill();
ctx.moveTo(113, 45);
// draw the right eye
ctx.arc(110, 45, 3, 0, Math.PI*2, true);
ctx.fill();
ctx.stroke(); // thicker eyes
```

I started a new path again, which means I can start drawing the arc for the eyes without using moveTo (as I did when making the smile). However, once I filled the arc, creating a solid-looking eye, I *lift* the pen with moveTo(113, 45) to draw the right eye. Notice that I moved to the right by the arc's first X coordinate plus the radius value to create a solid line, which ensures that the starting point of the arc matches where I put the pen down. Finally I use the stroke method to give the eyes a bit more thickness.

The code goes on to move the drawing point around and finally end up with an image of our stick man.

There's also a number of other path methods, which are beyond the scope of this chapter, that you can use for finer control over the lines and shapes you draw, including quadraticCurveTo, bezierCurveTo, arcTo, rect, clip, and isPointInPath.

Canvas and SVG: when to use which

Canvas and SVG are both very good drawing APIs, but for different reasons, and with anything, you want to use the right tool for the job. SVG is a *retained-mode API*, and the 2D canvas API is an *immediate-mode API*.

SVG maintains a tree that represents the current state of all the objects drawn onscreen, which makes it a retained-mode API. As this tree is available, it makes it a great candidate for interactivity because you can bind to specific objects in the tree and listen for click or touch events and even hit detection for games. It also has good support in desktop tools such as Adobe Illustrator and Inkscape for importing and exporting SVG graphics, rather than having to wrestle XML to create your image. SVG is vector based, so it handles scaling much better; canvas is a bitmap-based image—it doesn't scale, it just zooms.

If you need some convincing that SVG is the right tool for the job, have a look at Raphaël, the JavaScript library by Dmitry Baranovskiy (**http://raphaeljs.com**). It uses SVG exclusively and is able to create some very impressive drawings and animations.

Canvas is very well suited to lots of animations and highly JavaScript-centric applications. It's a lower-level API when compared to SVG, which means that it's better for when there *isn't* mouse interaction because there's no tree maintaining the state of the canvas. It is good for when you have keyboard interaction, like many of the 8-bit game demos that have emerged in the last year. Since canvas is JavaScript centric, in your processing loop you can handle keyboard events on the document level. Finally, canvas is pixel orientated, as illustrated in the stick man examples in Figure 5.10, so it's good for pixel pushing.

Each of these technologies has its strengths and weaknesses. As the developer, it's your job to understand the requirements of your application and pick the right one. Good luck!

Using transformers: pixels in disguise

As well as being able to move the pen around the canvas using methods like moveTo, drawing shapes and lines, you can also adjust the canvas *under* the pen using transformations.

Transformation methods include rotate, scale, transform, and translate (all similar to their CSS counterparts).

In **Figure 5.12**, I've drawn a spiral; the aim is to have it rotate in a circle, giving a quasi-twilight zone effect. Ideally I would keep the function that draws the spiral the same, not changing any positions, starting points, or anything else. This would keep the code much easier to manage. So to ensure that the spiral code remains simple, I can rotate the canvas under the pen, and then redraw the exact same spiral, except the result is rotated slightly in one direction.

The rotate method rotates from the top left (0, 0) position by default. This wouldn't do at all, and if I rotated the canvas from this position, the spiral would circulate offscreen, as if it was on a pendulum. Instead I need to rotate from the centre of the spiral, which I'll place in the centre of the canvas. Therefore I need to rotate from the centre of the canvas.

The translate method can help me here. It moves the 0, 0 coordinate to a new position. **Figure 5.13** shows that I've drawn a dot and also shows the arguments I passed to translate. Each time translate runs it sets the new coordinates to 0, 0.

FIGURE 5.13 Example of how translate can move the origin points of the canvas.

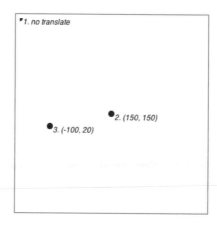

Now to achieve my rotating spiral I need to initialise the canvas using translate, and then use setInterval to redraw my spiral (note that drawSpiral is my own function, rather than native,

TIP The context object has an attribute called canvas, which has a back-reference to the canvas element it's part of. You can use this to go back to the canvas and read the height and width—useful for when you only have the context.

that draws the path for a spiral and uses stroke to draw it on the canvas):

```
ctx.translate(ctx.canvas.width/2, ctx.canvas.height/2);
drawSpiral(); // the complicated magic mathematics

setInterval(function () {
  ctx.clearRect(-ctx.canvas.width/2, -ctx.canvas.height/2,
              ctx.canvas.width, ctx.canvas.height);
  ctx.rotate(Math.PI / 180 * 0.5) // 1/2 a degree
  drawSpiral();
}, 10);
```

The only caveat I have to deal with is clearing the canvas. I would normally use clearRect(0, 0, width, height), but since translate has moved the 0, 0 position to the centre of the canvas, I need to manually specify the top left, as you see in the previous code listing.

Capturing images

As well as drawing lines and shapes, you can also copy images from other sources, specifically images, videos, and other canvas elements. I've already shown that you can use images as the source of a createPattern fill. You can also draw images straight onto your canvas. You can even crop images and manipulate the images as they are copied on.

Since you can capture an image from a video element, this makes for some interesting opportunities. There's already lots of demos out in the wild, including dynamically injecting content into video, green screen replacement for video, and facial recognition—all using combinations of canvas and video all written in JavaScript.

The capturing and drawing is done entirely through the drawImage method, which accepts the different HTML element sources mentioned before, and accepts the following three sets of arguments:

- drawImage(image, dx, dy)
- drawImage(image, dx, dy, dw, dh)
- drawImage(image, sx, sy, sw, sh, dx, dy, dw, dh)

where d is the destination position and s is the source. For example, if I took Bruce's synergies video from Chapter 4, and wanted to run a repeating thumbnail of him bashing the banana across the top of my web site, I could do it by cropping and scaling using the `drawImage` method.

The components I need are:

- A canvas fixed across the top of my site

- A *hidden* video running the synergies video

- A way to loop just the bit of the video I want

- A method to capture what's on the video and transfer it to the canvas

The reason I'm using a hidden video is because this will be the source for my canvas, but I don't want it to be seen. I just want to keep grabbing the video frame and putting it on the canvas.

I *just* want the part of Bruce smashing the banana with the mallet, so I need to tell the video just to play that part. There's no content attribute I can use to tell it to start from a particular point, I'm just going to force the `currentTime` to second 49. Then on the `timeupdate` event, I'll force the `currentTime` back to 49 if it goes above 52 seconds. So my time range is the window of 49 to 52 seconds in the video. Due to some browsers trying to hold back data and missing support for the `video.seekable` property, for this example I'm going to use a timer to try to force the start time:

```
var jumpTimer = setInterval(function () {
  try {
    // if the data isn't available, setting currentTime
    ¬will throw an error
    video.currentTime = start;
    clearInterval(jumpTimer);
    video.play();
  } catch (e) {}
}, 100);

video.addEventListener('timeupdate', function () {
  if (this.currentTime > 52) this.currentTime = 49;
}, false);
```

The previous code keeps trying to set the `video.currentTime` value, but doing so before the video data is ready throws a JavaScript error. If the error is thrown, the code doesn't reach `clearInterval`. If successful, the `setInterval` is cleared and the video is played.

Now that the video loop is in place, I can start grabbing frames from the video element. I *could* use the timeupdate event to draw the canvas, but I know that the effect doesn't perform anywhere nearly as well as if I run the canvas drawing in its own timer. I could speculate that this is because the browser is trying to do the hard work to render the video element; by separating it in a timer, it gives the browser some room to breathe.

Once the loadeddata event fires on the video, I'm going to initialise the canvas, so that it's the same width as the window (otherwise our image would stretch, as you saw in Figure 5.9). Then I'll mute the video (to avoid being too annoying!) and calculate the shortest edge because I want to crop a square from the video and repeat it across the canvas:

```
video.addEventListener('loadeddata', function () {
  var size = 78; // thumbnail size
  canvas.width = window.innerWidth;
  video.volume = 0;
  shortestEdge = video.videoHeight > video.videoWidth ?
    video.videoWidth :
    video.videoHeight;

  // kick off our drawing loop
  setInterval(function () {
    for (var i = 0, w = canvas.width; i < w; i += size) {
  // arguments have been broken into multi lines
      ctx.drawImage(
        video,
        (video.videoWidth - shortestEdge)/2, // sx
        (video.videoHeight - shortestEdge)/2, // sy
        shortestEdge, // sw
        shortestEdge, // sh
        i, // dx
        0, // dy
        size, // dh
        size // dy
      );
    }
  }, 67); // 67 is approximately 15fps
}, false);
```

All the magic is happening inside of the setInterval, which triggers every 67/1000th of a second (since JavaScript measures seconds by 1000 milliseconds; therefore 1000/15 = about 67, or approximately 15fps), which should be good enough for faking video playback. Once inside the setInterval, I'm looping over the width of the canvas, incrementing by the size of the thumbnail I'm drawing so as to fill the canvas horizontally.

The mapping for the arguments to the drawImage method is shown in **Figure 5.14**.

FIGURE 5.14 A visual representation of arguments passed to drawImage.

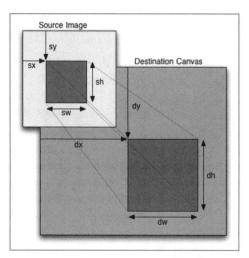

Using a simple crop for the height and width, and using the shortest edge, I can then easily scale the crop to the thumbnail size and let the canvas do all the hard work for me. The result: Bruce bashing a banana across the top of my site (**Figure 5.15**).

FIGURE 5.15 An animated banner across my site using canvas and video.

Pushing pixels

One very cool feature of the canvas API is its ability to interrogate individual pixels, something that isn't possible with the alternative drawing SVG technology. You can get every pixel from the 2D context object, broken down into four colour channels: red, green, blue, and the alpha transparency channel (rgba). For example:

```
var ctx = document.querySelector('canvas').
¬getContext('2d'),
    img = document.createElement('img');

// wait until the image has loaded to read the data
img.onload = function () {
  ctx.drawImage(img, 0, 0);
  var pixels = ctx.getImageData(0, 0, img.width,
  ¬ img.height);
};
```

> **NOTE** To use the source of another image in the **drawImage** method, it must be served through http (not a local file system).

The variable pixels is a CanvasPixelArray, which contains the height, width, and data properties. data is an array of the pixel data, which is made up as follows

```
[ r1, g1, b1, a1, r2, g2, b2, a2, r3, g3, b3, a3, ... ]
```

where r1, g1, b1, a1 makes up the first pixel, r2, g2, b2, a2 makes up the second pixel, and so on. This means that data.length is the number of pixels captured from the getImageData (in the previous example this will be the same size as the image) multiplied by 4, as there are 4 channels to each pixel.

Since you have access to this data, you can do pixel-level processing. So you *could* create custom image filters for applications like the image editors shown in Figure 5.2 or perhaps scan the image for particular colour ranges or even write a web app that does facial recognition.

Paul Rouget and Tristan Nitot of Mozilla showed off a demo early in 2009 (see **Figure 5.16**) that uses a video drawn on to a canvas and injects dynamic content in to the image seen on the canvas. As each video frame is drawn on to the canvas, the pixel data is read and searched for a solid block of white (where the pixel is 255, 255, 255), which is used as an anchor point to draw another visual element on to the canvas. In Figure 5.16, another canvas element has been dynamically injected. You can play with the demo here: **http://people.mozilla.com/~prouget/demos/DynamicContentInjection/play.xhtml.**

FIGURE 5.16 Scanning a video for bright pixels to inject dynamic content.

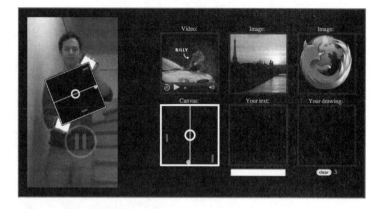

In the following code example, I load an image into the canvas and invert all the pixels, creating a strange x-ray version of Bruce and me (**Figure 5.17**):

```
var ctx = document.querySelector('canvas').
¬getContext('2d'),
    img = document.createElement('img');

// wait until the image has loaded
img.onload = function () {
  ctx.canvas.width = img.width;
  ctx.canvas.height = img.height;
  ctx.drawImage(img, 0, 0);
  var pixels = ctx.getImageData(0, 0, img.width,
  ¬img.height);

  for (var i = 0, n = pixels.data.length; i < n; i += 4) {
    pixels.data[i+0] = 255 - pixels.data[i+0]; // red
    pixels.data[i+1] = 255 - pixels.data[i+2]; // green
    pixels.data[i+2] = 255 - pixels.data[i+1]; // blue
    // i + 3 is the alpha channel which we don't need
  }
  ctx.putImageData(pixels, 0, 0);
};
img.src = 'authors.jpg';
```

In the previous code listing, I wait until the image has loaded before trying to copy it to the canvas. I draw it in to the canvas and immediately read out the pixel data to make my invert adjustment to the pixels.

In the `for` loop, I'm using `i += 4`, which ensures I'm iterating over *each pixel* and not the pixel channels. By setting the pixel bit to 255 minus the current value, I get an inverted colour.

Finally, I put the pixels variable back in to the canvas after making my changes using `putImageData`, passing in the `CanvasPixelArray` object and the x/y start point.

FIGURE 5.17 If you were to x-ray Bruce and Remy, you'd see they look just as strange.

> **NOTE** The canvas element contains an internal origin-clean flag that's set to true by default. This flag will flip to false if an image or video is used whose origin does not match that of the document that owns the canvas. The same goes for using a canvas as an image source if it already has the origin-clean flag set to false. If the flag is false, it means that you won't be able to use the `getImageData` or `toDataURL` methods. This remains the case even if you change the size of your canvas or draw on the canvas after the flag is set to false.

Saving to file

You've made the next best thing since sliced bread? Want to save your beautiful drawing to your desktop? You want to export it in multiple formats? No problem. Canvas has you covered.

The canvas element (*not* the 2D context) supports exporting the current state of the canvas to a data URL.

What's a data URL?

Most browsers support being able to read base64 encoded assets, such as an image. The URL scheme looks like this:

data:image/png;base64,iVBORw0KGgoAAAANSUhEUgAAAAoAAAAK...etc

It starts with data, then the mime type, then the encoding, base64, and then the raw data. This raw data is what's exported by the canvas element, and browsers are able to decode the data in to real assets (sadly, this doesn't include IE7 or previous incarnations of IE). In addition, IE8 only supports data URLs up to a length of 32Kb—something to watch out for!

Exporting is very easy. The canvas has the toDataURL method, which can be invoked with the format in which you want your image. Only PNG support is required by the canvas specification, but browsers can support other types if they choose. For example, Safari supports GIF, PNG, and JPG. Trying to get the data URL for an unsupported TIFF format returns exclusively the letter "A" multiple times and no data:<mime-type>. Opera supports only PNG, but on requesting a JPG or GIF, it still returns a PNG (ignoring the file format). Firefox (on a Mac) supports only PNG, throwing an error on all other types (which is a little severe if you ask me). The lesson here is that once you have your data URL back, ensure that it starts with data:*<your-mime-type>* to ensure that they match up and the return format is what you asked for.

The following example generates a similar drawing from the *hello world* drawing and immediately saves it to a PNG by redirecting the browser to the rendered image:

```
var ctx = document.querySelector('canvas').
¬getContext('2d');
ctx.fillStyle = 'rgb(0, 0, 255)';
ctx.fillRect(0, 0, ctx.canvas.width, ctx.canvas.height);
ctx.fillStyle = 'rgb(0, 255, 0)';
ctx.fillRect(10, 20, 50, 50); // little square
window.location = ctx.canvas.toDataURL('image/png');
```

Finally, the toDataURL also takes an optional second argument that is available only if image/jpg has been implemented to allow you to specify quality level of the image generated. This value would be between 0.0 and 1, with 1 being the highest quality available, and it affects the size of the base64 data generated from toDataURL.

Animating your canvas paintings

You've already seen some basic animations using canvas throughout this chapter, but I wanted to explain some of the concepts in detail here.

Animation is very basic and manual on a canvas. If there's an area that you want to animate, you must draw, clear the area, draw again, and rinse and repeat.

The Processing JavaScript Library

As you'll find out, it's a blast to navigate around the canvas with a pen drawing lines and filling shapes, but there are already some libraries available that make working with the canvas much easier. One of these such libraries is called processing.js (**http://processingjs.org/**), written by the author of jQuery, John Resig.

It's not actually a library designed to ease working with canvas, but it in fact interprets the Processing language in JavaScript, which is in turn drawn on the canvas element. In many ways, processing.js is a great tool for visualisation and abstracts away a lot of the more complicated drawing and animation procedures in the 2D drawing API.

Simple animation is mostly about clearing the current canvas state and drawing the whole thing again. As the canvas is a native drawing API, it's very quick to do so. I'll show you a demo that takes Bruce's bouncy head and bounces it around the canvas area. This example is based on the canvas breakout tutorial by Bill Mill, but I jazzed it up with Bruce's mug bouncing instead of a solid black ball.

The code used for **Figure 5.18** is relatively simple and breaks down into the following tasks:

1.   initialise the canvas and objects I want to draw

2.   clear the canvas

3.   draw the ball on the canvas

To add extra spice, I rotate Bruce's face in circles whilst he bounces around. So I'll have to do some rotation on the canvas, too.

FIGURE 5.18 While away the
hours whilst you watch Bruce's
face bounce around a canvas
animation.

Since I'm going to rotate Bruce's face, I'm going to let *another*
canvas handle that task (so that I can keep my main canvas free
from rotation and translations). This way it keeps my tasks simple in that in one canvas I'm rotating an image of Bruce; in the
second, I'm working out the position of his face on the canvas
and drawing it there.

```
var ctx = document.querySelector('canvas').
¬getContext("2d"),
    ballctx,
    x = 100, // arbitrary start points
    y = 50,
    dx = 2,
    dy = 4,
    width = ctx.canvas.width,
    height = ctx.canvas.height;

// load the image
ballImg = document.createElement('img');
ballImg.src = 'bruce-ball.png';

// once loaded, start the ball bouncing
ballImg.onload = function () {
  var ball = document.createElement('canvas');
  ball.height = 50;
  ball.width = 50;

  ballctx = ball.getContext('2d');
```

```
// translate to centre to rotate properly
ballctx.translate(25, 25);

setInterval(draw, 10);
};


function draw() {
  ctx.clearRect(0, 0, width, height);

  ballctx.rotate(Math.PI/180*5); // 5 degrees

  // draw at the 0,0 position
  ballctx.drawImage(ballImg, 0, 0, ballImg.width,
  ¬ballImg.height, -25, -25, 50, 50);

  // copy the rotated source
  ctx.drawImage(ballctx.canvas, x, y);

  if (x + dx > width || x + dx < 0)
    dx = -dx;
  if (y + dy > height || y + dy < 0)
    dy = -dy;

  x += dx;
  y += dy;
}
```

All the action is happening in the draw function, but only after I've finished setting up. The setup dynamically creates the ball canvas, hides it (because I don't need it to be seen on the page—it's just a utility for the effect), and translates the canvas so that the rotation happens in the centre of the canvas. From the code you can see I've created a new canvas element, but not put it inside the DOM. I can still use the 2d context but only if I set the height and width. If I don't do this, the height and width defaults to zero, which means there's no area to paint to or to get pixels out of that, whereas, if you insert the canvas into the DOM, it automatically gets a width of 300px and height of 150px.

The draw function then runs every 1/100th of a second (10 milliseconds), constantly incrementing the x and y position and redrawing the ball canvas onto the main canvas, but not before the blanket *clearing* of the canvas with `ctx.clearRect(0, 0, width, height)`, which is effectively resetting the entire effect.

So that's it. Animation. Probably most akin to a flip-book animation.

Saving and restoring drawing state

There is a little more hope built in to the 2D API: drawing state. There are two methods on the context object: save and `restore`, which manage the current stack of drawing states. The save method *pushes* the current state on to the stack, whereas restore *pops* from the top of the stack.

Drawing states don't cover *everything* you do to the canvas, but they do include the following:

- Transformations

- Clipping regions (not covered in this book)

- The current values for the following attributes: `fillStyle`, `font`, `globalAlpha`, `globalCompositeOperation`, `lineCap`, `lineJoin`, `lineWidth`, `miterLimit`, `shadowBlur`, `shadowColor`, `shadowOffsetX`, `shadowOffsetY`, `strokeStyle`, `textAlign`, and `textBaseline`.

For example, the following code snippet from the Mozilla canvas composition tutorial shows how it would draw 50 stars on a canvas in random positions. It sets the position using the `translate` method. But at the end of each iteration of the loop, it restores the original state of the canvas, thus moving the top/left of the canvas to the real top left, rather than in the position of the last `translate`:

```
for (var j=1;j<50;j++){
  ctx.save();
  ctx.fillStyle = '#fff';
  ctx.translate(75-Math.floor(Math.random()*150),
                75-Math.floor(Math.random()*150));
  drawStar(ctx,Math.floor(Math.random()*4)+2);
  ctx.restore();
}
```

Note that save and restore do not affect the current paths or current bitmap on the canvas (you can't restore to a previous state of the image on the canvas).

Rendering text

The canvas allows you to render text on to the canvas and specify fonts, sizes, alignment, and baselines. You can also fill text (as normal text might appear) and stroke text (for example, around the outline). Bespin (**https://bespin.mozillalabs.com**) is a great example of how custom text rendering can be used to create a fully functional code editor entirely written using the canvas API.

Drawing text requires the string and coordinates. For example, to show you how to use translate, I used an annotated canvas (shown in **Figure 5.19** and also earlier in this chapter in Figure 5.13). I used fillText to annotate the new centre point of the canvas to label the dots I had placed around the canvas (whose height and width are hard coded to 300x300 for this example):

```
function dot(string) {
  ctx.beginPath();
  ctx.arc(0,0,5,0,Math.PI*2,true); // draw circle
  ctx.fill();
  ctx.fillText(string, 5, 10); // render text
}
```

Now I can translate the canvas and call the dot function, passing the string I want printed next to the dot:

```
dot('1. no translate'); // show dot
ctx.translate(150, 150);
dot('2. (150, 150)'); // show dot
ctx.translate(-100, 20);
dot('3. (-100, 20)'); // show dot
```

FIGURE 5.19 Using fillText to annotate a canvas.

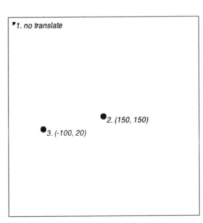

By default, the `fillText` method uses 10px sans-serif as the selected font. You can change this to your own font style by setting the font property on the context using the same syntax as CSS fonts (for example, `ctx.font = 'italic 400 12px/2 helvetica neue, sans-serif'`). When I call `fillText`, the text rendering uses the same `fillStyle` that I set earlier (or uses the canvas default). Equally `strokeText` uses `strokeStyle`.

Accessibility within the canvas element

One reason that canvas is so fast on today's optimised *JIT* JavaScript interpreters is that it keeps no DOM. So, if you need any kind of collision detection, for example, you need to do all the bookkeeping yourself. There is no representation that JavaScript can interrogate.

This also causes difficulty for accessibility. If your games are keyboard- *and* mouse-accessible, that goes a long way to meeting the needs of many. But for users with visual impairments, there is nothing for assistive technology to hook into. Canvas text is the same: bringing text into canvas means it ceases to be text and is just pixels. It's even worse than `<img>` because at least that can take alt text. Although the contents of the element (the text between the canvas tags) can be changed with script to reflect the canvas text you're inserting with JavaScript, I'm not optimistic that developers will do this.

An accessibility task force of the HTML Working Group is looking at ways to enhance the accessibility of canvas. It's not impossible; Flash 5 managed to add accessibility features. However, I recommend that for the time being, canvas shouldn't be used for user interfaces or the only way to communicate information. Something like the Filament Group's jQuery Visualize plug-in is a good example of canvas being used to supplement accessible information. It uses jQuery to inject a canvas element to a page that graphs the information from a data table that's in the markup. Assistive technologies have access to the raw data table, while the information is supplemented with visual graphs for sighted users.

Summary

The canvas API finally brings a native drawing device to the browser without the need to paint through a Flash app. The canvas is especially powerful for pixel-level processing, and I can imagine that canvas-based applications will be pushing the boundaries of what we've historically seen on the web.

However, you should be careful to choose the right technology for the job. SVG should definitely be considered before ploughing ahead with your next Awesome 3.0 app.

CHAPTER 6

Data Storage

Remy Sharp

STORING DATA ASSOCIATED with an application is fundamental in nearly all applications, web or desktop. This can include storing a unique key to track page impression, saving usernames, preferences, and so on. The list is endless.

Up until now, storing data in a web app required you either to store it on the server side and create some linking key between the client and the server—which means your data is split between locations—or it would be stored in cookies.

Cookies suck. Not the edible ones, the ones in the browser. They're rubbish. There's a number of issues with cookies that make working with them a pain. On starting any new project that requires cookies, I'll immediately go hunting for my cookie JavaScript library. If I can't find that, I'll head over to Google to find Peter-Paul Koch's cookie code, and copy and paste away.

> **NOTE** Peter-Paul Koch's cookie code: http://www.quirksmode.org/js/cookies.html

> **NOTE** The only saving grace of cookies, and what makes them work, is the fact that they're shared with the server via a request header. This can be used to help prevent security exploits; otherwise, in most cases, I've found web storage kicks a cookie's butt!

Looking at how cookies work, they're overly complicated. Setting a cookie in JavaScript looks like this:

```
document.cookie = "foo=bar; path=/";
```

That's a session-based cookie. Now, if I want to store something for longer, I'll have to set it in the future, and give it a specific lifetime (and if I want it to persist, I'll have to keep setting this to be *n* days in the future):

```
document.cookie = "foo=bar; path=/; expires=Tues,
¬13 Sept 2010 12:00:00";
```

The time format is important too, which only causes more headaches. Now, the icing on the horrible-tasting cookie: To delete a cookie, I need to set the value to blank:

```
document.cookie = "foo=; path=/";
```

In fact, the cookie isn't *really* deleted, it's just had the value changed and had the expiry set to a session, so when the browser is shut down. Delete should really mean delete.

Cookies don't work because they're a headache. The new storage specifications completely circumvent this approach to setting, getting, and removing data by offering a clean API.

Storage options

There are two options when it comes to storing data on the client side:

- Web Storage—supported in all the latest browsers
- Web SQL Databases—supported in Opera, Chrome, and Safari

Conveniently, Web SQL Databases is so named to instantly give you a clue as to how it works: It uses SQL-based syntax to query a local database.

Web Storage is a much simpler system in which you simply associate a key with a value. No learning SQL required. In fact, support for the Web Storage API is much better than for Web SQL Databases. I'll look at both of these APIs, how they work, and how to debug data in each system.

As a guidance for space, Web Storage typically has a limit of 5Mb (but Safari, for instance, will prompt users if more than 5Mb is used, and ask whether they want to allow the website to go beyond the current default).

On the other side of the fence, the Web SQL Databases specification doesn't talk about limits, and it's up to the author to try to gauge an idea of the total size of the database when it's created.

In both cases, the browser will throw an error if the API wasn't able to write the data, but I'll focus on smaller applications where the data stored is around the 100Kb mark.

Web Storage

In a nutshell, the Web Storage API is cookies on steroids. One key advantage of this API is that it splits session data and longterm data properly. For contrast, if you set a "session" cookie (that is, one without expiry data), that data item is available in all windows that have access to that domain until the browser is shut down. This is a good thing, because the session should last the time the window is open, not the browser's lifetime. The storage API offers two types of storage: sessionStorage and localStorage.

> **NOTE** Cookies on steroids vs. regular cookies: IE6 supports only 20 cookies per domain and a maximum size of 4K per cookie. Web Storage doesn't have a maximum number of items that can be stored per domain, and it limits the aggregate size to upwards of 5Mb.

If you create data in sessionStorage, it's available only to that window until the window is closed (for example, when the session has ended). If you opened another window on the same domain, it wouldn't have access to that session data. This is useful to keep a shopping session within one window, whereas cookies would let the session "leak" from one window to another, possibly causing the visitor to put through an accidental additional transaction.

localStorage is based around the domain and spans all windows that are open on that domain. If you set some data on local storage it immediately becomes available on any other window on the same domain, but also remains available until it is explicitly deleted either by you as the web author or by the user. Otherwise, you can close your browser, reboot your machine, come back to it days later, and the data will still be there. Persistent data without the hassle of cookies: having to reset the expiry again and again.

Watch out for Firefox cookie security

Firefox implements slightly different security around access to session and local storage: If cookies are disabled, accessing `sessionStorage` or `localStorage` will throw a security error. In this case, you need to check whether you're able to set cookies before trying to access either of these two storage APIs.

```
var cookiesEnabled = (function () {
  // the id is our test value
  var id = new Date().getTime();

  // generate a cookie to probe cookie access
  document.cookie = '__cookieprobe=' + id + ';path=/';

  // if the cookie has been set, then we're good
  return (document.cookie.indexOf(id) !== -1);
})();
```

This code tries to set a cookie and then immediately read it back again. If it fails to read the cookie, it means that security is blocking you from writing and therefore you can't access the `sessionStorage` or `localStorage`. If cookies aren't enabled, the implications are that reading from `sessionStorage` or `localStorage` will cause a security warning and break your JavaScript.

An overview of the API

Since both the `sessionStorage` and `localStorage` descend from the Web Storage API, they both have the exact same API (from the specification):

```
readonly attribute unsigned long length;
getter DOMString key(in unsigned long index);
getter any getItem(in DOMString key);
setter creator void setItem(in DOMString key, in any data);
deleter void removeItem(in DOMString key);
void clear();
```

This API makes setting and getting data very easy. The `setItem` method simply takes a key and a value. The `getItem` method takes the key of data you want and returns the content, as shown here:

```
sessionStorage.setItem('twitter', '@rem');
alert( sessionStorage.getItem('twitter') ); // shows @rem
```

It's worth noting that in all the latest browsers the `getItem` doesn't return "any" data type. The browsers convert the data type to a string regardless of what's going in. This is important because it means if you try to store an object, it actually stores "[Object object]". More importantly, this means numbers being stored are actually being converted to strings, which can cause errors in development.

To highlight the possible problems, here's an example: Let's say that Bruce runs a website selling videos of himself parading as a professor of science. You've added a few of these videos to your shopping basket because you're keen to learn more about "synergies." The total cost of your shopping basket is $12, and this cost is stored in sessionStorage. When you come to the checkout page, Bruce has to add $5 in shipping costs. At an earlier point during your application, $12 was stored in sessionStorage. This is what your (contrived) code would look like:

```
sessionStorage.setItem('cost', 12);
```

```
// once shipping is added, Bruce's site tells you the total
¬ cost:
function costWithShipping(shipping) {
 alert(sessionStorage.getItem('cost') + shipping);
}
```

```
// then it shows you the cost of the basket plus shipping:
costWithShipping(5);
```

> **NOTE** Where the specification said we could store "any data," we can actually store only DOMString data.

If sessionStorage had stored the value as a number, you would see an alert box showing 17. Instead, the cost of $12 was saved as a string. Because JavaScript uses the same method for concatenation as it does for addition (for example, the plus symbol), JavaScript sees this as *appending* a number to a string—so the alert box actually shows 125—much more than you'd probably be willing to pay to watch any video of Bruce! What's going on here is *type coercion*, whereby upon storing the data in the storage API, the data type is coerced into a string.

With this in mind, the API is (currently) actually:

```
readonly attribute unsigned long length;
getter DOMString key(in unsigned long index);
getter DOMString getItem(in DOMString key);
setter creator void setItem(in DOMString key, in DOMString
¬ data);
deleter void removeItem(in DOMString key);
void clear();
```

Finally, it's worth noting that if the key doesn't exist when you call getItem, the storage API will return null. If you're planning on using the storage API to initialise values, which is quite possible, you need to test for null before proceeding because it can throw a pretty nasty spanner in the works if you try to treat null as any other type of object.

Ways to access storage

As we've already seen, we can use setItem and getItem to store and retrieve, respectively, but there are a few other methods to access and manipulate the data being stored in the storage object.

Using expandos

Expandos are a short and expressive way of setting and getting data out of the storage object, and as both sessionStorage and localStorage descend from the Web Storage API, they both support setting values directly off the storage object.

Using our example of storing a Twitter screen name, we can do the same thing using expandos:

```
sessionStorage.twitter = '@rem';
alert( sessionStorage.twitter ); // shows @rem
```

Unfortunately the expando method of storing values also suffers from the "stringifying" of values as we saw in the previous example, with Bruce's video website.

Using the key method

The API also provides the key method, which takes an index parameter and returns the key associated. This method is useful to enumerate the data stored in the storage object. For example, if you wanted to show all the keys and associated data, you wouldn't particularly know what the keys were for each of the data items, so loop through the length of the storage object and use the key method to find out:

```
for (var i = 0; i < sessionStorage.length; i++) {
  alert( sessionStorage.key(i) + '=' +
  ¬ sessionStorage.getItem( sessionStorage.key(i) ) );
}
```

Another word of warning: It's conceivable that you might be storing some value under the name of "key," so you might write some code like the following:

```
sessionStorage.setItem('key',
¬ '27152949302e3bd0d681a6f0548912b9');
```

Now there's a value stored against the name "key," and we already had a method called key on the storage object: Alarm bells are ringing, right?

Some browsers, WebKit specifically, overwrite the key method with your new value. The knock-on effect is the developer tools in WebKit make use of the key method to enumerate and display all the data associated with the storage object—so the "Storage" view for that storage type (sessionStorage, in our example) will now be broken until that value has been removed.

> **NOTE** I expect that as the browsers continue to develop, this kind of bug will be crushed—but in the meantime I'd say do your very best to avoid using names that already exist on the storage API.

Other browsers such as Firefox will keep the key method and your key value stored separately. Using the expando syntax will give you the method, and using getItem('key') will give you the value.

Removing data

There are two ways to remove data from the storage object programmatically: removeItem and clear. The removeItem method takes a key, the same key used in setItem and getItem, and deletes the entry for that particular item.

Using clear removes all entries, clearing the entire storage object. For example:

```
sessionStorage.setItem('bruce', "Think he's a professor of
¬ synergies");
sessionStorage.setItem('remy', "Think Bruce is a loony
¬ professor of synergies");
alert( sessionStorage.length ); // shows 2
sessionStorage.removeItem('bruce');
alert( sessionStorage.length ); // show 1
sessionStorage.clear();
alert( sessionStorage.length ); // shows 0
```

Storing more than strings

NOTE JSON (JavaScript Object Notation) is a text based open standard for representing data. The specification found at **http://json.org** is so simple it actually fits on the back of a business card!

You can work around the "stringifying" of objects by making use of JSON. Since JSON uses text to represent a JavaScript object, we can use this to store objects and convert stored data back into objects, but it's really a wrapper for this bug. It depends whether the browsers intend to support the *any data* storage eventually, but this is easy to test for. However, it would require putting a wrapper on the set and get methods, which (depending on your application) may or may not be an option.

All the latest browsers (either nightly or final releases) support native JSON encoding using the JSON.parse and JSON.stringify methods. For those browsers that don't have JSON support, we can include Douglas Crockford's JSON library (available at **http://www.json.org/json2.js**).

Now you can wrap setItem and getItem as follows:

```
var videoDetails = {
  author: 'bruce',
  description: 'how to leverage synergies',
  rating: '-2'
};

sessionStorage.setItem('videoDetails', JSON.
¬ stringify(videoDetails) );

// later on, as in page reloads later, we can extract the
¬ stored data
var videoDetails = JSON.parse(sessionStorage.getItem
¬ ('videoDetails'));
```

As I stated in the API overview section, if the key doesn't exist in the storage object, then it will return null. This isn't a problem for the native JSON parsers as JSON.parse(null) returns null—as you would expect. However, for Douglas Crockford's JavaScript version, passing null will throw an error. So if you know it's possible that Douglas' JSON JavaScript library is being loaded, protect against this error by using the following:

```
var videoDetails = JSON.parse(sessionStorage.getItem
¬ ('videoDetails') || 'null');
```

This ensures that if null is returned from the getItem method, you pass in a JSON-encoded version of null, and thus the JavaScript based JSON parser won't break.

Using debugging tools

Although there's good support for the Web Storage API, the debuggers are still maturing. So aside from introspecting the `sessionStorage` or the `localStorage` there's not too many tools available.

WEBKIT'S DEVELOPER TOOLS

> **NOTE** To enable the Developer menu in Safari, go to Preferences and from the Advanced tab, check the Show Developer Menu in Menu Bar box.

Whilst I refer to WebKit, in this section I'm covering Safari, the nightly build of Safari (WebKit), and Google Chrome. WebKit's developer tool allows us to view the `localStorage` and `sessionStorage` values stored as shown in **Figure 6.1**. From here you can modify keys and values and delete entries.

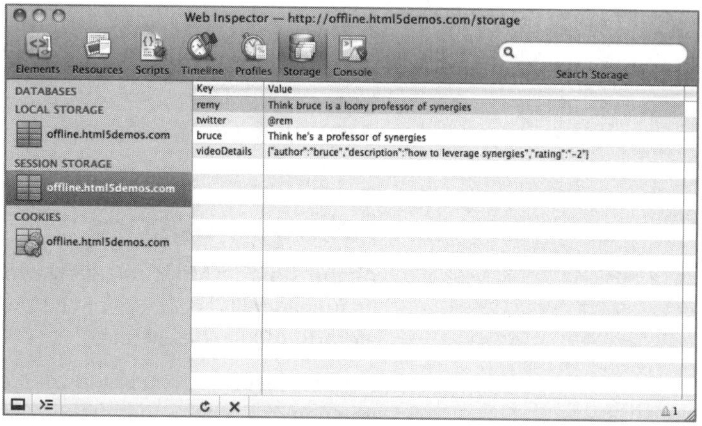

FIGURE 6.1 WebKit's storage debugger.

FIREFOX'S FIREBUG

Using the Firebug plugin for Firefox you can easily introspect the storage objects. If you enter "sessionStorage" or "localStorage" in the console command and execute the code, the storage object can now be clicked on and its details can be seen (**Figure 6.2**).

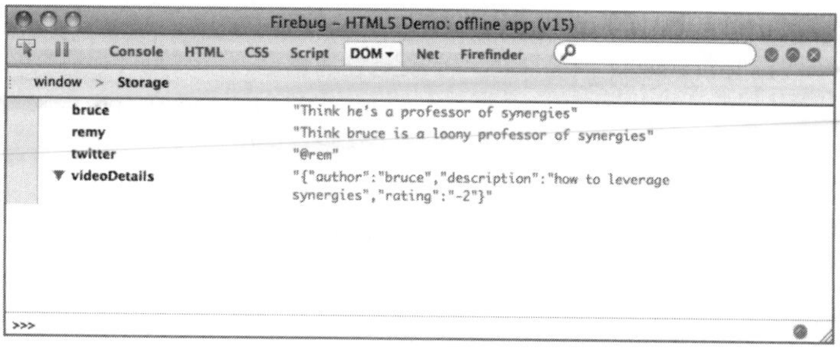

FIGURE 6.2 Firebug's storage introspector.

OPERA'S DRAGONFLY

DragonFly comes shipped with Opera, and from the Storage tab you can access all the data stored in association with the current page. In particular, there are separate tabs for Local Storage and Session Storage to inspect all the data linked with those data stores (**Figure 6.3**).

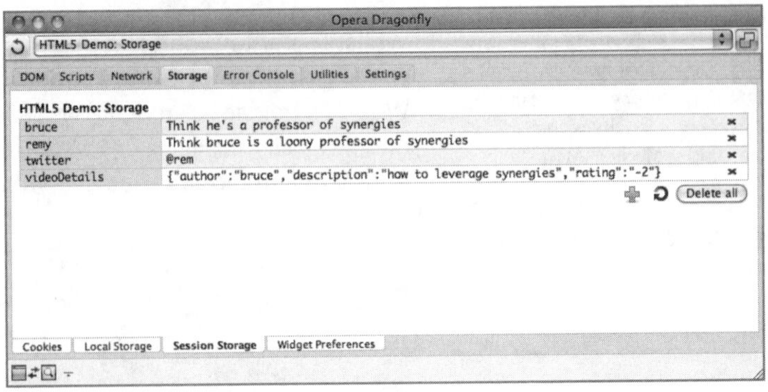

FIGURE 6.3 Opera's DragonFly debugger to inspect storage.

Fallback options

As the storage API is relatively simple, it's possible to replicate its functionality using JavaScript, which could be useful if the storage API isn't available.

For `localStorage`, you could use cookies. For `sessionStorage`, you can use a hack that makes use of the `name` property on the `window` object. The following listing shows how you could replicate `sessionStorage` functionality (and ensure the data remains locked to the current window, rather than leaking as cookies would) by manually implementing each of the Storage API methods. Note that the following code expects that you have JSON support in the browser, either natively or by loading Douglas Crockford's library.

```
if (typeof sessionStorage === 'undefined') {
  sessionStorage = (function () {
    var data = window.top.name ? JSON.parse(window.top.
    ¬name) : {};

    return {
      clear: function () {
```

```
          data = {};
          window.top.name = '';
        },
        getItem: function (key) {
          return data[key] || null;
        },
        key: function (i) {
          // not perfect, but works
          var ctr = 0;
          for (var k in data) {
            if (ctr == i) return k
            else ctr++;
          }
        },
        removeItem: function (key) {
          delete data[key];
          window.top.name = JSON.stringify(data);
        },
        setItem: function (key, value) {
          data[key] = value+''; // forces the value to a
          ¬ string
          window.top.name = JSON.stringify(data);
        }
      };
    })();
}
```

The problem with implementing sessionStorage manually (as shown in the previous code listing) is that you wouldn't be able to write sessionStorage.twitter = '@rem'. Although technically, the code would work, it wouldn't be registered in our storage object properly and sessionStorage.getItem('twitter') wouldn't yield a result.

With this in mind, and depending on what browsers you are targeting (that is, whether you would need to provide a manual fallback to storage), you may want to ensure you agree within your development team whether you use getItem and setItem.

Web SQL Databases

> **NOTE** Mozilla and Micro-
> soft are hesitant about
> implementing SQL database
> support. Mozilla is looking at a
> specification called Indexed
> Database API which is only in
> early betas of Firefox 4 and is
> beyond the scope of this chap-
> ter. But it's worth keeping an
> eye on it in the future.

Web SQL Databases are another way to store and access data. As the name implies, this is a real database that you are able to query and join results. If you're familiar with SQL, then you should be like a duck to water with the database API. That said, if you're not familiar with SQL, SQLite in particular, I'm not going to teach it in this chapter: There are bigger and uglier books that can do that, and the SQLite website is a resource at **http://sqlite.org**.

The specification is a little bit grey around the size limits of these databases. When you create a new database, you, the author, get to suggest its estimated maximum size. So I could *estimate* 2Mb or I could estimate 20Mb. If you try to create a database larger than the default storage size in Safari, it prompts the user to allow the database to go over the default database size. Both Opera and Google Chrome simply allow the database to be created, regardless of the size. I strongly suggest that you err on the side of caution with database sizes. Generally, browsers are limiting, by default, databases to 5Mb per domain. Now that you're suitably worried about SQL and database sizes, one really neat feature of the Web SQL Databases API is that all the methods allow you to pass a callback that will be executed once the fandango SQL magic has completed. Callbacks are a common trait of JavaScript libraries such as jQuery. If you're not familiar with this syntax, it looks something like what follows (but don't worry, I'll hold your hand throughout the examples later on):

```
transaction.executeSql(sql, [], function () {
  // my executed code lives here
});
```

Due to the nature of the callback system, it also means that the database API is *asynchronous*. This means you need to be careful when authoring the JavaScript to deal with the database to ensure that the sequence of events runs correctly. However, the SQL statements are queued and run in order, so this is one slight advantage you have over processing order: You can create tables and know that the table will be in place before you run queries on the tables.

Put plainly, if you want your code to run after the database interaction has completed, use the callback. If you don't need to wait, and you want your code to continue regardless, continue after the database API call.

> ### Be very wary of versioning!
>
> Currently, the implementations of Web SQL Databases support a slightly older version of the Web SQL Databases API, and more specifi-cally the versioning model.
>
> Although the specification describes how you can manage and migrate from different versions of the database, this hasn't been implemented very well. The model requires that you know the version of the data-base on the user's machine to be able to open it. The problem is that if you have migrated through multiple versions of your database, there's no way to determine which version the visiting user is on, and opening the database with the wrong version number throws an `INVALID_STATE_ERROR`. You could wrap each of the open database attempts in a try/catch, but you'd require one for each version of your database, something that could get very messy after a few years of upgrades.

Using the Web SQL Database API

The typical database API usage involves opening the database and then executing some SQL. Note that if I were working with a database on the server side, I would typically close the data-base connection. This isn't required with the database API, and in fact there's no method to do this at all. That all said, you *can* open a database multiple times.

Opening and creating databases

By opening a database for the first time, the database is cre-ated. You can only have one version of your named database on the domain at any one time, so if you create version 1.0 you can't then open 1.1 without the database version having been specifically changed by your application. For the rest of this chapter, I'm going to ignore versioning and stick to one version only due to the previously stated warning.

```
var db = openDatabase('mydb', '1.0', 'My first database',
¬2 * 1024 * 1024);
```

The latest version of the SQL databases spec includes a fifth argument to openDatabase, but this isn't supported in any of the browsers right now. It offers a callback when the database is created for the first time. You've now created a new data-base called "mydb," version 1.0, with a text description of "My first database," and you've set the size of the data to 2Mb (this

has to be set in bytes which is why I multiply 2 * 1024 * 1024).
To ensure our app works and detects support for the Web SQL
database API, you should also test for database support in the
browser, so you wrap our code with the openDatabase test:

```
var db;
if (window.openDatabase) {
  db = openDatabase('mydb', '1.0', 'My first database',
  ¬2 * 1024 * 1024);
}
```

It's as simple at that. The next thing to do is set up a new table
in the database, which will go through the exact same methods
as selecting and updating tables: via executeSql.

Creating tables

With creating tables (and any other transaction on the database),
you must start a database "transaction" and, within the callback,
create the table. The transaction callback receives an argument
containing the transaction object, which is the thing that allows
you to run SQL statements and run the executeSql method (tx in
the following example). This is done using the database object
that was returned from openDatabase and calling the transaction
method as so:

```
var db;
if (window.openDatabase) {
  db = openDatabase('tweetdb', '1.0', 'All my tweets',
  ¬2 * 1024 * 1024);
  db.transaction(function (tx) {
    tx.executeSql('CREATE TABLE tweets (id, date, tweet)');
  });
}
```

The executeSql method takes four arguments, of which only the
first is required:

1. SQL

2. Arguments to SQL (such as field values)

3. Success callback

4. Error callback

In the previous example, you only use the SQL parameter. Of course if the statement to create a table runs and our table already exists there's actually an error being triggered, but since you're not catching it and it doesn't affect our program flow, in this instance you don't care.

However, the next step of this application is to load the database with tweets from Twitter, and this has to happen once the table is in place (because of the asynchronous nature of the Web SQL Database API), you'll have to get the tweets in the complete callback. Herein lies a problem: If the table exists, the transaction will fail and won't trigger the success callback. The code will run fine the first time around, but not the second. So to get around this, you'll say to only create the table if the table doesn't exist; this way the success callback fires if the table is created and if the table already exists, and the error callback is only called if there's some other problem.

```
var db;
if (window.openDatabase) {
  db = openDatabase('tweetdb', '1.0', 'All my tweets',
  ¬ 2 * 1024 * 1024);
  db.transaction(function (tx) {
    tx.executeSql('CREATE TABLE IF NOT EXISTS tweets
    ¬ (id, date, tweet)', [], function () {
      // now go and load the table up with tweets
    });
  });
}
```

Inserting and querying

Now let's say you hit Twitter for a search query for all the mentions of HTML5, you store all those tweets in your database, then you allow the user to select the time range of tweets from the past 5 minutes, 30 minutes, 2 hours, and then all time. The time range selection will be radio buttons with click handlers, and you'll run your query to show only the tweets from that time range.

The crux of this application is split between storing the tweets in your database and showing the tweets depending on the time range.

Before any of your code runs, first you must create the database and tweets table, which will include a date column whose type is integer—which is important to allow you to query the database later on in your application:

```
function setupDatabase() {
  db = openDatabase('tweets', '1.0', 'db of tweets',
  ¬2 * 1024 * 1024);
  db.transaction(function (tx) {
    tx.executeSql('CREATE TABLE tweets (id unique,
    ¬screen_name, date integer, text)');
  });
  getTweets();
}
```

A few things to note about the code are:

1. I'm using a global db variable. (I'm just using a global for the contrived example; global is generally bad in JavaScript.)

2. I'm telling the tweets database that the id column is unique. This means if there's a duplicate INSERT attempt, the INSERT fails.

3. If the CREATE TABLE fails, it's fine because it will only fail because the table already exists, and you're not doing anything else in that transaction.

4. Once it's done, I call getTweets, which will make the API request to Twitter, which will in turn call the storing function.

> **NOTE** You're creating a new transaction for each stored tweet, I'll explain transactions in more detail in the next section, but by wrapping individual INSERT statements you're ensuring that all the new tweets are stored, irrespective of whether you already have these in the database.

The forEach method in the following code is a new JavaScript method available in all the latest browsers, allowing you to loop through an array. Mozilla's site provides simple code for implementing this in browsers that don't have it natively: **https://developer.mozilla.org/en/Core_JavaScript_1.5_ Reference/Global_Objects/Array/forEach**. Once the Twitter API call completes it will call saveTweets, which will do the storing of each of the tweets:

```
function saveTweets(tweets) {
  tweets.results.forEach(function (tweet) {
    db.transaction(function (tx) {
      var time = (new Date(Date.parse(tweet.created_at))).
      ¬getTime();
      tx.executeSql('INSERT INTO tweets (id, screen_name,
      ¬date, text) VALUES (?, ?, ?, ?)', [tweet.id,
      ¬tweet.from_user, time / 1000, tweet.text]);
      // div 1000 to get to seconds
    });
  });
}
```

The INSERT statement is the most important part, and now you can see how the field arguments work:

```
tx.executeSql('INSERT INTO tweets (id, screen_name, date,
¬text) VALUES (?, ?, ?, ?)', [tweet.id, tweet.from_user,
¬time / 1000, tweet.text]);
```

Each "?" in the INSERT statement maps to an item in the array that is passed in as the second parameter to executeSql. So the first "?" maps to tweet.id, the second to tweet.from_user, and so on.

You can also see that I've divided the time by 1000; this is because JavaScript time goes to milliseconds, whereas SQLite doesn't. SQLite goes down to whole seconds. This is only important for your query later on in the code where you show tweets that are 5 minutes old. This matters because you're storing dates as integers, and one second using JavaScript's getTime method gives us 1000, whereas one second using SQLite gives us 1. So you divide by 1000 to store seconds rather than milliseconds.

Finally, when the radio buttons are clicked, you call the show function with the amount of time as the argument:

```
var tweetEl = document.getElementById('tweets');
function show(amount) {
  db.transaction(function (tx) {
    tx.executeSql('SELECT * FROM tweets' + (amount !=
    ¬'all' ? ' WHERE date > strftime("%s", "now", "-' +
    ¬amount + ' minutes")' : ''), [], function
    ¬(tx, results) {
      var html = [],
          len = results.rows.length;

      for (var i = 0; i < len; i++) {
        html.push('<li>' + results.rows.item(i).text +
        ¬'</li>');
      }
      tweetEl.innerHTML = html.join('');
    });
  });
}
```

On initial review this code may look complicated, but there are actually only a couple of things happening here:

1. Start a new transaction

2. Run a single SQL statement, whose structure is determined by whether you want "all" or not

3. Loop through the results constructing the HTML, and then set it to the tweetEl (a `<ul>` element) innerHTML

There's two states the SQL query can be, either:

```
SELECT * FROM tweets
```

or

```
SELECT * FROM tweets WHERE date > strftime("%s", "now",
¬ "-5 minutes")
```

Where I've put -5 minutes, this can change to -30 minutes or any number that's passed in to the show function. The `strftime` SQLite function is generating the number of seconds from 1-Jan-1970 until "now" minus *N* minutes. Since the "date" field is being stored as an integer, you're now able to grab all the rows that were tweeted within the last *N* minutes.

Now you've used the third argument to the executeSql method, the success callback. The success callback receives a transaction object (just as the transaction callback does so you could run another executeSql if you wanted), and more importantly, the result set. The result set contains three attributes:

1. insertId (set only if you've inserted a row or rows)—I didn't use this in this example.

2. rowsAffected—Since this is a SELECT statement, this value is 0.

3. rows—This *isn't* an array, it's a collection, that *does* contain a length and item getter method. You make use of the rows object, and run a for loop from 0 to the length of the rows, and use `results.rows.item(i)` to get the individual rows. The individual row is an object representing the different column names, so `results.rows.item(0).screen_name` gives us the screen_name field from the first row.

Finally, once you have looped through all the rows that match, you can set a `<ul>` element to the HTML you've built up. In this example, the `<ul>` is stored in the variable called tweetEl.

Here is the complete code listing, which includes the database support detection and the click handler code for the radio buttons:

```
<!DOCTYPE html>
<html lang="en">
<head>
<meta charset=utf-8 />
<title>HTML5 tweet time range</title>
```

```
<style>
  body { font-family: helvetica, arial;}
</style>
</head>
<body>
  <form>
    <fieldset>
    <legend>Select a time range of recent HTML5 tweets</
    ¬ legend>
    <input type="radio" value="5" id="t5m" name="timerange"
    ¬ /><label for="t5m">5 minutes</label>
    <input type="radio" value="30" id="t30m" name=
    ¬ "timerange" /><label for="t30m">30 minutes</label>
    <input type="radio" value="120" id="t2h" name=
    ¬ "timerange" /><label for="t2h">2 hours</label>
    <input type="radio" value="all" id="tall" name=
    ¬ "timerange" checked="checked" /><label for="tall">
    ¬ all time</label>
    </fieldset>
  </form>
  <ul id="tweets"></ul>
<script>
var tweetEl = document.getElementById('tweets');
var db;

function setupDatabase() {
  if (!window.openDatabase) {
    tweetEl.innerHTML = '<li>Web SQL Database API is not
    ¬ available in this browser, please try nightly Opera,
    ¬ Webkit or Chrome.</li>';
    return;
  }
  db = openDatabase('tweets', '1.0', 'db of tweets',
  ¬ 2 * 1024 * 1024);
  db.transaction(function (tx) {
    tx.executeSql('CREATE TABLE tweets (id unique,
    ¬ screen_name, date integer, text)');
  });
  getTweets();
}

function getTweets() {
  var script = document.createElement('script');
```

```
      script.src = 'http://search.twitter.com/search.
      ¬json?q=html5 -RT&rpp=100&callback=saveTweets';
      document.body.appendChild(script);
    }

    // our Twitter API callback function
    function saveTweets(tweets) {
      tweets.results.forEach(function (tweet) {
        db.transaction(function (tx) {
          var time = (new Date(Date.parse(tweet.created_at))).
          ¬getTime();
          tx.executeSql('INSERT INTO tweets (id, screen_name,
          ¬date, text) VALUES (?, ?, ?, ?)', [tweet.id,
          ¬tweet.from_user, time / 1000, tweet.text]);
          ¬// divide by 1000 to get to seconds
        });
      });
    }


    function show(amount) {
      db.transaction(function (tx) {
        tx.executeSql('SELECT * FROM tweets' + (amount !=
        ¬'all' ? ' WHERE date > strftime("%s", "now", "-" +
        ¬amount + ' minutes")' : ''), [], function
        ¬(tx, results) {
          var html = [],
              len = results.rows.length;

          for (var i = 0; i < len; i++) {
            html.push('<li>' + results.rows.item(i).text +
            ¬'</li>');
          }
          tweetEl.innerHTML = html.join('');
        });
      });
    }

    // bind the click handlers for the radio buttons
    [].forEach.call(document.querySelectorAll('input
    ¬[type=radio]'), function (el) {
      el.onclick = function () {
        show(this.value);
      }
```

```
});

// go!
setupDatabase();

</script>
</body>
</html>
```

Creating transactions— and what they're good for

I've skipped over transactions so far. They're more than meets the eye. They're not just the way to run queries; they serve a particularly useful purpose. Transactions are like closed environments in which you can run your queries. You can run just one query or a group of queries within a transaction. In fact, you *can't* run a query *without* being inside a transaction, since the executeSql method is *only* available from the SQLTransaction object.

Possibly the most important aspect of the transactions is this: If something fails inside the transaction (vanilla code or SQL statements), then the whole transaction is rolled back. This means it's as if the whole transaction block of code never happened.

The transaction method takes two arguments: The first is the contents of the transaction; the second, optional, is the error handler if it's triggered. Below is a contrived example that shows you how a transaction will rollback your failed transaction:

```
var db = openDatabase('foo', '1.0', 'foo', 1024);
db.transaction(function (tx) {
  tx.executeSql('CREATE TABLE foo (id unique, text)');
  tx.executeSql('INSERT INTO foo (id, text) VALUES
  ¬ (1, "foobar")');
});

db.transaction(function (tx) {
  tx.executeSql('DROP TABLE foo');

  // known to fail - so should rollback the DROP statement
  tx.executeSql('INSERT INTO foo (id, text) VALUES
  ¬ (1, "foobar")');
}, function (error) {
  // error.message is "no such table: foo"
```

```
    alert('Rollback triggered, the table "foo" was never
    ¬dropped due to: ' + error.message);
});

db.transaction(function (tx) {
  tx.executeSql('SELECT * FROM foo', [], function (tx,
  ¬results) {
    alert('found ' + results.rows.length + ' row');
  }, function (tx, error) {
    // this will never execute
    alert('something went wrong: ' + error.message);
  });
});
```

What you're doing in the previous code is:

1. Start a transaction that creates the table foo and then inserts a single row

2. Start a transaction that drops the table foo and then incorrectly tries to insert a new row in foo

3. This transaction will fail, and rollback the statements (that is, it's as if step 2 never happened)

4. Start a transaction that selects all the rows from foo and alerts the number of rows

5. The SQL query succeeds and shows "found 1 row"

Transactions are used to ensure an atomic block of queries execute and if any part fails, it rolls back.

Summary

In this chapter, you learned about two different APIs for storing data locally in the browser that beats the pants off using cookies (and there's more storage specs in the works with Indexed Database API).

These storage APIs allow you to store a lot more data than the traditional cookie and make the associated programming a lot easier than before. On top of which, the Web Storage API has really good support in all the latest browsers (and older browsers can be supported using JavaScript), so it means you can drop the awful and stale cookies of today!

CHAPTER 7

Offline

Remy Sharp

HOW MANY TIMES have I been working on a train, desperately trying to get a 3G connection with my cheap dongle, and failed to navigate the web application I was using because I've just traveled through a tunnel (and thus lost all connectivity)? A lot, that's how many. Computing either with no Internet or with a particularly choppy connection usually means mobile computing, but it can also mean you just want to work offline. Equally, the user may not have chosen to go offline. As we become more mobile with our computers, being able to continue to use a website outside of reception becomes more and more important.

We're used to creating web apps that rely absolutely on the Web. Our websites run in browsers, which are designed to be a viewport onto the Web. The offline web applications part of the HTML5 spec takes the "web" out of "web app." The browser will manage a local cache so our application will work without an Internet connection.

Pulling the plug: going offline

> **NOTE** In the context of the offline spec, the manifest is a list of files that define what files should be included for your offline application.

To work offline, an application needs only a *manifest* telling the browser what it needs to store in its local cache. The manifest can be as simple as a list of files and you'll be done. Once the browser has stored the cache of assets, CSS, JavaScript, images, etc., when the page is reloaded, the browser uses these local assets to drive the website.

Along with telling the browser what to cache, you can also tell it what *not* to cache, ensuring that requests to that particular URL always go via the Web. Finally, HTML5 gives you a way to manage fallback cases. In the situation where you're currently without a connection and you try to access a resource that isn't in your local (offline) cache, the fallback can be used to serve a *different* resource. For example, going to the chat part of your application could fall back to a page saying this feature is available only while online.

The first part of an offline application is down to the manifest, which tells the browser what to cache (or not to, in some cases). The second part is in the applicationCache. This object contains methods to trigger updates and to swap the latest cache into the browser. It also has events firing off of it that the author can use to notify the user that the application might be upgradable.

The cache manifest

The manifest is the thing that tells the browser when and what to get from offline, from the Web, or to fall back onto if assets are missing. Once the manifest is loaded or updated, it triggers an update on the applicationCache object. To tell the browser to look for a manifest is simple: You add the manifest attribute to the <html> element, and point it to the file containing your application's manifest:

```
<!DOCTYPE html>
<html lang="en" manifest="/time.manifest">
<!-- my awesome time app lives here -->
</html>
```

My example application, in all its glory, will show you the time on your machine and show you the time on my server. Not quite as complex as a Google Docs application, but enough to demonstrate that, when the connection isn't available, instead of showing the server time—which it can't get—it will show you the working app, but with the server time marked as unavailable. **Figure 7.1** shows the application on first load and whilst it's online.

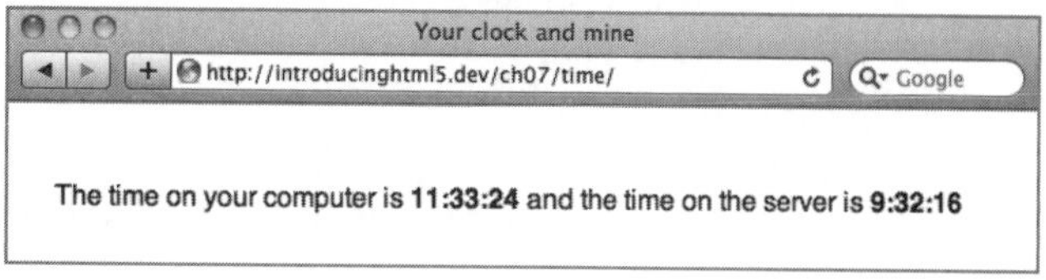

FIGURE 7.1 Move over, Google Apps: Our application tells us the time!

My complete application requires

- The application page: `index.html` in this case

- `time.js`: the code to tick the clock forward

- `time.css`: simple styles for my app

- `server-time.js`: In this example, let's say this is generated every minute by my server.

Everything, with the exception of the `server-time.js` file, will be stored in the manifest. Finally, in addition, I need a file that will be served up in place of `server-time.js` if we're offline. This will be

- `fallback-server-time.js`: contains a notice about being offline

Here's what the contents of my `time.manifest` look like:

```
CACHE MANIFEST
index.html
time.js
time.css

FALLBACK:
server-time.js fallback-server-time.js

# version 8
```

The format of the file is important. You'll see the first line is `CACHE MANIFEST`. This tells the browser that what follows is the source to a manifest file. Within the manifest, files are listed under categories, also known as namespaces. The default category is CACHE, and if it isn't stated, all the filenames encountered are put in that category until the browser hits a new category. So with that in mind, I could have written my file to look like the following—and it would have the exact same effect:

```
CACHE MANIFEST

CACHE:
index.html
time.js
time.css

FALLBACK:
server-time.js fallback-server-time.js

# version 9
```

NOTE The web page that includes the manifest (in the `<html>` tag) is also implicitly included in the cache manifest. For this reason, I recommend explicitly including the file, `index.html` in my case, in the manifest so that you don't get confused further along in the development of your project.

You can repeat a category, too. To append new files to be included in the cache, include them at the end of the file so the manifest reads: cache, fallback, cache. This is perfectly valid, too.

FALLBACK tells the browser that if anything matches the URL on the left, in my case server-time.js, and it's not in the manifest and it can't be accessed with the existing connection, then serve up the file specified on the right side, in my case fallback-server-time.js. The fallback file fallback-server-time.js is included in the files that are cached by the browser, just as files are in the CACHE category.

FALLBACK also allows you to use URL paths, so you could use the following:

```
FALLBACK:
server-time.js fallback-server-time.js
/ offline.html
```

This tells the browser that if server-time.js is requested and it's not available, then serve up fallback-server-time.js. If any other path is requested, such as /foo.html, and it's not available (either because you're offline or it's not in the cache), then serve offline.html. This technique could be used to allow your entire application to work offline and wall off the areas that require the web and notify your user via the offline.html page that they need to be online to access this particular section. **Figure 7.2** shows my time application when the app doesn't have connectivity to the site, and the request for server-time.js falls back to fallback-server-time.js showing an entirely different message.

FIGURE 7.2 My time application continues to work while offline, pulling a different resource for the server-time JavaScript file.

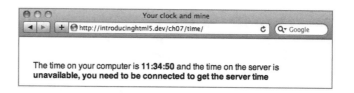

> **NOTE** Cachebusting means to use a forceful technique to prevent the resource from being cached. In the example of the manifest, this is achieved by changing its contents.

> **NOTE** Browsers like the manifest and don't let go of their cache easily. Make sure you include a comment that has a version number, revision, or timestamp that you can change and force an update to the browser's manifest.

Finally I've included a comment in the file, starting with the # symbol (note that comments must be on their own line, too). This tells me the version number. This is important to *cachebust* the manifest.

This doesn't have to be a number or anything in particular, but to tell the browser to reload the contents of the manifest you need to change the contents of the file, and not just the timestamp, to force a reload. I'm using a version number here, this could be a revision ID from your favourite revision control system, or it could be a datetime stamp, or something that's unique and changes when you need to reload.

In addition to the CACHE and FALLBACK categories, there's the NETWORK category, which I've not needed in my example. The NETWORK category is a "whitelist" category, telling the browser that all requests to files or paths in this category must go via the Web and must not be cached. For example

```
NETWORK:
live-time.php
/realtime-stuff/
```

tells the browser that it must be on the Web to access live-time.php but also anything that matches the absolute path of http://mysite.com/real-timestuff/. Equally, you can use the NETWORK category to explicitly state that anything that isn't cached must go via the web by using a wildcard * (note that this is the default behaviour if omitted):

```
CACHE MANIFEST
index.html
time.js
time.css


FALLBACK:
server-time.js fallback-server-time.js


NETWORK:
*


# version 10
```

How to serve the manifest

NOTE Changing the mime types on your web server is beyond the scope of this book, but get in touch with your hosting company and they will point you in the right direction.

There's one last hurdle to jump before you can take your application completely offline: You need to serve the manifest file properly, meaning it must have the extension `.manifest` and it must have the right mime-type.

If you're using a common web server like Apache, you need to add the following to your mime.types file:

```
text/cache-manifest manifest
```

This ensures that Apache is sending the `text/cache-manifest` file header when you request any file with the `.manifest` extension. You can test this by checking the headers of the file requested using a tool like `curl` and the `-I` (capital i):

```
curl -I http://mysite.com/time.manifest
```

That should return (something like) this:

```
HTTP/1.1 200 OK
Date: Thu, 04 Mar 2010 12:59:30 GMT
Server: Apache/2.2.13 (Unix) mod_ssl/2.2.13 OpenSSL/0.9.8l
¬DAV/2 PHP/5.3.0
Last-Modified: Mon, 01 Mar 2010 16:20:24 GMT
Accept-Ranges: bytes
Content-Length: 113
Content-Type: text/cache-manifest
```

Now that your server is sending the right headers, and your manifest file is ready to be used, pat yourself on the back. Let's take a look at it in action.

The browser-server process

When working with the offline applications, it's useful to understand the communication process between the browser and the server. If at all possible, I recommend running the following command on your servers to *tail* your access logs whilst refreshing your page using the cache manifest to see exactly what's being pulled. It will show you whether the files from your manifest are actually being requested and served up by your server:

```
tail -f logs/access_log
```

When you visit a web page that makes use of the cache manifest, such as my time example, here is what happens:

1. Browser: requests **http://introducinghtml5.com/examples/ch07/time/**

2. Server: returns `index.html`

3. Browser: parses `index.html` and requests all the assets in the page, images, CSS, JS, and the manifest file

4. Server: returns all requested assets

5. Browser: processes the manifest and requests all the items in the manifest, regardless of whether it's just requested them. This could effectively be a double request for your application if you're caching all the assets

6. Server: returns the requested manifest assets

7. Browser: application cache has updated, trigger an event stating so

Watch out for dodgy foxes!

Firefox boasts support for offline applications, but it doesn't work properly and has been historically buggy. If you're testing with Firefox, make sure you're also checking what's actually being requested from your server by monitoring the server logs. In particular, the manifest should be requested once the browser is using the cache manifest. Currently Firefox 3.6 doesn't request the manifest, meaning that you're stuck on that version of your code, which is bad! There is hope! You can tell the browser never to cache the manifest file by adding the following code to your server config or `.htaccess` (or similar) file:

If you're using `mod_expires` for Apache, you need to include the following in your `httpd.conf`:

```
<IfModule mod_expires.c>
  ExpiresActive on
  ExpiresByType text/cache-manifest "access plus 0 seconds"
</IfModule>
```

You also send custom headers on requests for .manifest files and send a `no-cache` header:

```
Header set Pragma "no-cache"
```

Now the browser has fully loaded the cache using the files listed in the manifest. If the manifest hasn't changed and the browser is reloaded, here's what happens:

1. Browser: re-requests **http://introducinghtml5.com/examples/ch07/time/**

2. Browser: detects that it has local cache for this page and serves it locally

3. Browser: parses `index.html`, and all assets in the local cache are served locally

4. Browser: request the manifest file from the server

5. Server: returns a 304 code notifying the browser that the manifest hasn't changed

Once the browser has its cache of assets, it serves them locally first and then requests the manifest. As shown in **Figure 7.3**, Safari is loading all the assets for my time application, but at the same time I'm monitoring the access log for the app, which we can see *only* `time.manifest` and `server-time.js` is being requested over the connection.

FIGURE 7.3 Safari makes a request for the app loading using the local cache and requesting only the manifest and server-time from the server. This time, you re-request the app—but the manifest has changed. If the manifest has changed, the process from step 1 to 4 is exactly the same, but next the browser needs to reload the cache.

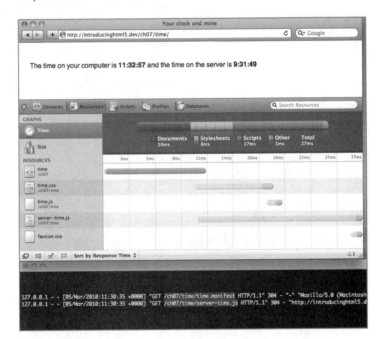

1. Browser: re-requests **http://introducinghtml5.com/examples/ch07/time/**

2. Browser: detects that it has local cache for this page and serves it locally

3. Browser: parses `index.html`, and all assets in the local cache are served locally

4. Browser: request the manifest file from the server

5. Server: returns the updated manifest file

6. Browser: processes the manifest and requests all the items in the manifest

7. Server: returns the requested manifest assets

8. Browser: application cache has been updated, trigger an event stating so

However, it's important to know that even though the assets may have changed, any previously loaded assets will not have changed (for example, images don't suddenly change, and old JavaScript functions haven't changed). In fact, at this point in the application's life, none of the new cache is available. Only when the page is reloaded will the new cached assets come into play and become available.

We'll look at how we can get our hands on these new assets by looking at the applicationCache object.

applicationCache

The applicationCache is the object that notifies you of changes to the local cache, but also allows you to manually trigger an update to the cache. Only if the manifest has changed will the applicationCache receive an event saying it has updated.

In the process list from the previous section, once the browser has finished loading the cache with the files from the manifest, the update event fires on the applicationCache. You could use this event to tell users that the application they're using has been upgraded and they should reload the browser window to get the latest and greatest version of your app. You can do this using a simple event listener and a notification:

```
applicationCache.onUpdateReady = function () {
  // the cache manifest has changed, let's tell the user to
  // reload to get whizz bang version 2.0
  notifyUserOfUpgrade();
};
```

However, what if you wanted to tell the user what had changed? Or even perhaps try to dynamically reload some portion of functionality. Strictly speaking, it's possible, but it might be tricky depending on your application. Nonetheless, to load the newly downloaded cache into memory, you can use the applicationCache.swapCache() method:

```
applicationCache.onUpdateReady = function () {
  applicationCache.swapCache();

  // the cache manifest has changed, let's tell the user to
  // reload to get whizz bang version 2.0
  notifyUserOfUpgrade();
};
```

Although swapping the cache removes the old cache and loads in the new cache, it doesn't actually swap images or reload any of our code. This only happens if the asset is manually reloaded or the entire window is reloaded. However, you could force a manual reload on one of these assets by dynamically creating a new DOM node for a script or image you wanted to reload.

For example, let's say that you have a file in your manifest that has the latest version description in version.js. If the browser has an upgrade ready (that you detected through the update ready event), inside the notifyUserOfUpgrade function you'll load the version.js file. Loading this file re-executes the JavaScript that's inside the version.js file and you'll be able to show users the latest list of changes if they reload the application.

I think that, generally speaking, the swapCache has very limited practical use. But the update ready event is very useful to tell users that they might want to reload the browser to get the updated application code, a bit like a normal desktop application telling us there's a new upgrade ready to be downloaded. Except in this case, the upgrade has already been downloaded behind the scenes for us.

Using the manifest to detect connectivity

Part of HTML5 includes a property on the navigator object that is *supposed* to tell you if the browser is online or offline, via

navigator.onLine

However, this property only changes via the application's menu and toggling "Work Offline" (in Opera, IE, and Firefox). This doesn't seem like a very good way to switch modes, so you can use the cache manifest's FALLBACK category to detect connectivity. By including a FALLBACK rule in our manifest, you can pull in a piece of JavaScript and detect whether you're online or offline.

Your manifest:

CACHE MANIFEST

FALLBACK:
online.js offline.js

online.js contains:

setOnline(true);

offline.js contains:

setOnline(false);

In your application you have a function called testOnline that
dynamically creates a script element that *tries to load* the
online.js JavaScript file. If it succeeds, the setOnline(true)
code is run. If you are offline, behind the scenes the browser
falls back on the offline.js JavaScript file, which calls
setOnline(false). From there, you might want to trigger the
applicationCache.update:

```
function testOnline(fn) {
  var script = document.createElement('script')
  script.src = 'online.js';

  // alias the setOnline function to the new function that was
  // passed in
  window.setOnline = function (online) {
    document.body.removeChild(script);
    fn(online);
  };

  // attaching script node trigger the code to run
  document.body.appendChild(script);
}

testOnline(function (online) {
  if (online) {
    applicationCache.update();
  } else {
    // show users an unobtrusive message that they're
    ¬ disconnected
  }
});
```

Killing the cache

As I mentioned earlier in this chapter, the browsers get pretty sticky with the cache. It's easy to get stuck in a cycle where you can't clear the cache to test a change you've made. So far, the spec doesn't have a method to programmatically clear the cache (for example, you can't do it from the applicationCache object).

With that in mind, during development I strongly urge you to avoid using the cache manifest. Make sure your application development is completely finished, and only then move on to adding the manifest attribute. That said, once you've got the cache in place, how do you go about clearing it?

Manually. Upgrading to a new cache should be as simple as changing the contents of the manifest file. As I said before, use a comment that includes a version number or similar. What if you want to start again, or what if you want to remove the manifest attribute all together? You'll only be able to do this during development because it requires you to clear the browser's cache (and depending on the browser, it's tucked away in different places).

> **NOTE** When you clear the cache, make sure there aren't any windows still open with your application that uses the manifest.

For WebKit-based browsers, you need to empty (or clear) the cache. By *cache* I mean anything that's been stored to help your browsing experience go faster. By *WebKit*, I mean Safari desktop, Safari mobile, and Chrome.

WebKit clears the cache for everything except that particular window, so when you refresh, it's still got the cache manifest included. This goes for the iPhone, too.

For Firefox, you need to open the preference, go to the Advanced tab, and select the Network tab. From there you can clear individual domains cache.

Summary

In the past, websites often failed to work when users weren't connected to the Internet. Browsers are now beginning to support this capability, and this chapter showed you how to make your web apps work without the web.

CHAPTER 8

Drag and Drop

Remy Sharp

SO WE'VE COME to the black sheep chapter of our book: Drag and Drop. It's not a black sheep in that cool way, like Darth Vader's version of the Imperial Tie Fighter; no, sadly it's the black sheep like you want to leave it alone in the field, and let it do its own thing. Some better men have even worse things to say about the spec.

So why is it here? Why is it in the HTML5 spec—and yes, drag and drop actually is part of the real HTML5 spec. Well, it's here because Microsoft Internet Explorer added drag and drop back in 1999 in IE5—yep, that long ago. Since then, Safari had implemented IE's API, so Ian Hickson, the HTML5 editor, reverse engineered the API, did all the hard work to understand exactly what was going on (describing the MSDN documentation as having a "*vague hand-wavy description*"), and documented the API.

> **NOTE** Details of Ian's investigation can be seen here: http://ln.hixie.ch/?start= 1115899732&count=1.

Now we're in the position where Firefox, Safari, Chrome, and IE support this API. It's not a good API—in fact, it's probably the worst API—but it's got some implementations so it's worth understanding what it's capable of.

Throughout this chapter, you'll be forgiven for crying out "WTF?" as we wind our way through rabbit's warren that is the drag and drop API. Why are we even including a chapter on this topic? It's because there is some interesting functionality that can be achieved from the API. The API, as the name implies, allows you to drag items and drop them anywhere in the browser. But this functionality is not limited to the browser. You can drag elements *from* the browser *to* external applications—like another browser window, or Photoshop, or a text editor—and the application can prepare the dragged data so that it's compatible with the drop target. This lends itself very well to the idea that HMTL5 is a Web Applications spec, and is giving us developers more functionality that borrows from desktop computing.

Getting into drag

We're going to start with the absolute minimum required to achieve the wonder that is dragging and dropping. By default, all links, text nodes (or selections of), and image elements are draggable. This means that you don't have to do anything to tell the browser they can be dragged around the page.

Our simple demo will have a drop zone and a couple of images that you can drag into the drop zone. And when you drop them, the image source will appear in the drop zone (see **Figure 8.1**).

FIGURE 8.1 All images and links are draggable by default. With a little more code, you can make them droppable too.

Since there's nothing to be done to the draggable images, you just need to hook up the drop zone, which requires the following event handlers:

1. Drag over: Tell the browser *this* is an element that accepts drop data.

2. On drop: Once *something* has been dropped on the element, do something with the dropped data.

I'm explaining the absolute minimum required to achieve drag and drop, but this method is only going to work in Safari. I'll then walk you through the tweaks required to get it to work in Firefox, Chome, and IE.

The other thing worth mentioning is that the specification up on **http://dev.w3.org/html5/spec/editing.html#dnd** says that there are *three* events you need to handle drag and drop. That isn't the case, or certainly not when it comes to practice. You need three events to get it working in all browsers, but not in Firefox and Safari.

Let's put all these caveats aside for a minute and crack on with our demo. The following listing is the über minimalistic source you need to see the drag and drop API in action:

```
<!DOCTYPE html>
<title>Simple drag demo</title>
<style>#drop { height: 100px; border: 5px solid #ccc; }
</style>
<img src="http://img.tweetimag.es/i/rem" alt="@rem" />
<img src="http://img.tweetimag.es/i/brucel" alt="@brucel" />
<div id="drop"></div>
<script>
  var drop = document.getElementById('drop');
  drop.ondrop = function (event) {
    this.innerHTML += '<p>' + event.dataTransfer.
    ¬ getData('Text') + '</p>';
  };
  drop.ondragover = function () { return false; };
</script>
```

I'm using the minimal HTML required just to keep things short. You can see from the previous code that I'm grabbing a reference to the div#drop element and then setting two inline event handlers: ondrop and ondragover.

When *something* is dropped on the drop element, it triggers the drop event and you're able to read the event.dataTransfer object. The default data type is *Text*, so you can use the getData method and ask for the text data type. In the case of an image, the text will be the source of the image (typically IE gives us null for the Text data type, but you'll fix that later). For links the href is the set data and for plain text that's been selected and dragged, the text itself is the set data.

Here's where it starts to get a little strange. To tell the browser that the drop element can accept items being dropped on it, you need to *cancel* the dragover event. Since I'm using an inline event handler (namely oneventname) I can return false. This prevents the default browser action. What *is* the default action? It's unclear from the spec, but it would be fair to say the default action would be to leave the object in the control of the browser. If I were using addEventListener, I would have to use event.preventDefault().

So that you're completely clear—because, frankly, it's not terribly obvious—here's a quote from the spec:

> *"If the drop is to be accepted, then this event (dragover) has to be canceled."*

So now that you've got your first drag and drop working, what about those tweaks I mentioned? Let's fix Firefox first; this is easy. When you drop the image on the drop zone in Firefox, it actually redirects the browser off to the value of getData('Text') for you if it looks like a link—that is, image sources and link hrefs. So that's easy: In the drop event, you prevent the browser's default action. If you're using inline handlers, you'll return false, or event.preventDefault(), so our drop handler now looks like this:

```
drop.ondrop = function (event) {
    this.innerHTML += '<p>' + event.dataTransfer.getData
    ¬('Text') + '</p>';
    return false;
};
```

Now, IE. Getting it working in IE isn't actually as painful as it could be. This is most likely because *they* came up with the API in the first place. IE doesn't listen to the dropover event, it listens for the dropenter event—and it's *this* event you need to cancel for IE to play ball. So let's add another event handler and return false, too. Since you're doing the same thing, I've created a function to return false:

```
function cancelEvent() { return false; }
drop.ondragenter = cancelEvent;
drop.ondragover = cancelEvent;
```

Again, since you're making it work in IE, IE doesn't pass in the event object to our inline handler, so you need to change the drop event handle to grab the global event object if you didn't receive one:

```
drop.ondrop = function (event) {
  event = event || window.event;
  this.innerHTML += '<p>' + event.dataTransfer.getData
  ¬ ('Text') + '</p>';
  event.cancelBubble = true;
  return false;
};
```

You also need to cancel the event from bubbling up the DOM to prevent new windows opening. Typically return false should handle this (as it does in the other browsers), but IE needs a helping hand with event.cancelBubble=true.

One final issue to fix: When you drop the image in IE or Chrome, you get "null" as the text in our drop zone. To fix this you need to set some data under the Text data type once the element starts to drag, using the dragstart event:

```
var imgs = document.getElementsByTagName('img'),
    i = imgs.length;
while (i--) {
  imgs[i].ondragstart = function (event) {
    event = event || window.event;
    event.dataTransfer.setData('Text', this.getAttribute
    ¬ ('alt'));
  };
}
```

Now you can see that I've set some data whose type is "Text" based on the alt attribute on the image. Now when the image is dropped, and the Text data type is read, you'll get the Twitter screen names instead of the image source. This drag and drop demo works in IE5 onwards, Firefox, Chrome, and Safari. More importantly, it's the setData method that really shows off the possibilities of the drag and drop model, but equally exposes some potential issues in the specification.

Interoperability of dragged data

By using the setData and getData methods on the dataTransfer object, you can pass data from elements inside our application to other pages of our app, or across browser windows—as 280 Slides has prototyped, when dragging one slide from one window to another completely separate document (**Figure 8.2**). Finally you can also accept or send data to native desktop applications.

FIGURE 8.2 An early prototype of how drag and drop could work in 280 Slides.

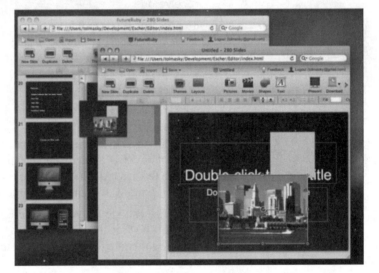

Dragging data to other applications

So long as you know what the accepted content types are, you can set the data type to that content type, and when you drag content from your application to that application. For example, on a Macintosh, the desktop accepts text snippets to be dragged onto it. I can construct my own content, set the content type to text/plain, and when I drag to the desktop (using Chrome or Safari), a text snippet is created with my content (**Figure 8.3**):

```
img.ondragstart = function (event) {
  event = event || window.event;
  // here be one long line
  event.dataTransfer.setData('text/plain',
    'This is the screen name for ' + this.getAttribute
    ¬('data-screen_name') +
    ', whose image can be found here: ' + this.src);
};
```

FIGURE 8.3 Dragged content from my web page creates a desktop text snippet.

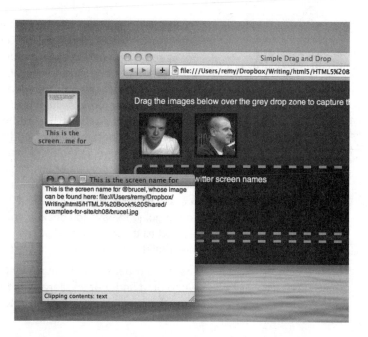

One final note about setData: It only accepts strings. This means you can't store a "complex" JavaScript object in a content type. However there's an easy enough solution around this: JSON.stringify.

All the latest browsers ship with native JSON encoding (stringify) and decoding (parse), so you can stringify our complex object and set it against a content type. For the older browsers you can include the JSON library from **http://json.org/json2.js** (though host it yourself as there's a nice little alert box you'll need to remove that prevents hotlinking), which will plug support for JSON stringify and parse.

Problems with setting drag data

Native desktop applications have had drag and drop for some time now and have had years to get the APIs right. One huge advantage that native applications have is that the setting of data doesn't actually happen, or execute, when the user starts dragging. It happens when the user drops.

There is an important reason for this: When you drop, you only need one content type.

> **NOTE** In total, there are seven drag and drop events. You've seen **dragenter**, **dragover**, **drop**, and **dragstart**. In addition there is **dragend** (the complement to **dragstart**) and **dragenter** and **dragleave**. The enter and leave events fire on the drop-zone as the dragged item enters the element.

Having to construct the different content types on the dragstart event makes you perform possibly unnecessary code execution. For example, if I were to allow the user to drag a canvas element to Photoshop, I would want to encode it as a Photoshop-compatible file and store it in the correct content type. But what if I'm also supporting *other* formats along with Photoshop? I'd have to do *all* that encoding at the point in which the dragstart event fires, but the user will, at best, only drop it on a single application. What if they're just dragging the element around to play? You've still run all that execution, a huge waste of processing for more complicated applications. If your application is simple, you may not see any performance issues; but if it's a fully fledged application, you're going to have to consider your options. Perhaps you don't support all those formats. Perhaps you only support one compatible format. Perhaps you don't even support drag and drop.

There are proposals to fix this (along with proposals to scrap the entire drag and drop model and start again), but for the medium term, this is a problem you'll have to work around.

How to drag *any* element

This is where the HTML5 spec added some new content to the API. Enabling *any* element to be dragged is incredibly easy. Take your div and add the new attribute: draggable. For example:

```
<div draggable="true">This element be draggable</div>
```

Of course I said *incredibly*. Well, it works in Firefox; any element that has the draggable attribute can now be dragged around the browser. Of course, since it's a new addition in HTML5, it doesn't come as standard in IE, so forget about it working in IE. Perhaps it will work in IE9 or later. More incredible is getting it to work in Safari 4.

Although it's blindingly simple to enable any element to be draggable using the draggable attribute, for reasons that are still beyond this author and many other bloggers, to get any element to drag in Safari 4 you need to give it a specific CSS style. That's right, to enable a *behaviour* you need to define a *presentational* attribute. This has been fixed in Safari 5 so the CSS isn't required, but for it to work in older Safari versions, you need the CSS. You must add the following CSS to target elements with the draggable attribute:

```
[draggable] { -webkit-user-drag: element; }
```

This uses the CSS attribute selector (the square brackets) to find all the elements with the property enabled, and then applies the behaviour to enable the user to drag the element.

Aside from the CSS fudge that you have to add to kick Safari 4 into life, dragging any element isn't too hard, and it means you can now create complicated objects in the DOM that the user can move around and drop into other windows or applications.

Adding custom drag icons

You can add your own custom drag icon when dragging an element. On the dragstart event, you can use the setDragImage method to associate your own image with the cursor at a specific offset to the cursor.

There's, of course, a small caveat: It doesn't work in IE, and in Safari, you can't override the cursor if dragging text, images, or links. But we're optimistic—let's create our own custom drag icon:

```
var dragIcon = document.createElement('img');
// set the drag icon to the mini twitter logo
dragIcon.src = 'http://img.tweetimag.es/i/twitter_m';
// later in the code...
element.ondragstart = function (event) {
  event.dataTransfer.setDragImage(dragIcon, -10, -10);
  // and do some other interesting stuff with dataTransfer
};
```

The result is a nice little bespoke drag icon that better represents the data you're moving around (**Figure 8.4**).

FIGURE 8.4 We've created a custom Twitter cursor when dragging Twitter-related data around.

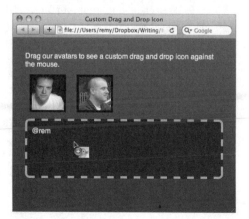

Accessibility

If you've made it this far undeterred by the warnings and dead bodies throughout this specification, then hopefully the application with drag and drop that you're implementing will come under the question of accessibility. Is the drag and drop API accessible, or can I make it accessible?

Well, as you'd expect with this specification, there's a good intention. So yes, the API has been designed with accessibility in mind. It's not terribly clear, but latest thinking is that the user should be able to control dragging and dropping using the keyboard copy and paste model.

The process is supposed to be: Navigate to the element you want to drag, copy to the clipboard using the keyboard shortcuts, then navigate to the drop zone, and paste using the keyboard.

As you've probably already guessed, no browser has implemented this (yet).

However, you can prepare your drag and drop demos to include ARIA support. You will need to set ARIA attributes on dragstart to indicate that the element is being dragged. We also need to now bind to the dragend event to remove the ARIA attribute. We should also use visual cues to indicate to the user what elements can be dragged and *where* they can be dropped. I'm not going to cover this detail, but Gez Lemon wrote a detailed article on adding ARIA and general accessibility to nonnative drag and drop, where the practises still apply to native drag and drop: **http://dev. opera.com/articles/view/accessible-drag-and-drop/**

```
var drop = document.getElementById('drop'),
    boxes = document.getElementsByTagName('div'),
    i = boxes.length;

while (i--) {
  if (boxes[i].getAttribute('draggable') != undefined) {
    boxes[i].ondragstart = function (event) {
      event = event || window.event;
      this.setAttribute('aria-grabbed', 'true');
      // set the drop targets up for ARIA support
      drop.tabIndex = 0; // for keyboard support
```

```
        drop.setAttribute('aria-dropeffect', 'copy');

        // then do something fancy with dataTranfer.setData
    };

    boxes[i].ondragend = function () {
        this.setAttribute('aria-grabbed', 'false');

        // reset the drop targets
        drop.tabIndex = -1; // for keyboard supportZ
        drop.removeAttribute('aria-dropeffect');
    };

    boxes[i].tabIndex = 0; // for keyboard support
    boxes[i].setAttribute('aria-grabbed', 'false');
  }
}
```

In the previous code, you're searching for the divs that have the draggable attribute. Then you add the ARIA support starting in the dragstart event. Once the element begins to drag, you set the aria-grabbed attribute to true, so that an assistive device can feedback. You're also now making the drop zone an element that can accept keyboard focus using tabIndex = 0 and finally you're saying the drop effect should be 'copy'. You could mirror the allowedEffect and dropEffect in the native drag and drop, but for now you'll remain focused on the ARIA support.

Next, you add the new dragend event handler, and once the element is no longer being dragged, you remove the aria-grabbed attribute and reset the drop zone attributes, i.e. no tabIndex and no dropEffect. Lastly, you initialise the draggable element, by setting the tabIndex and the grab flag.

With this completed code, your users can move around your application and its drag and drop components and their screen-readers (if they support ARIA) will feed back the current state of the operation.

However—and this is a big *however*—since no browser has implemented the keyboard support for drag and drop, you will most likely have to consider rolling your own drag and drop using JavaScript to handle everything (instead of relying on the native drag and drop functionality)—a rather sad ending to what is a particularly common operation on the web.

Summary

The drag and drop API isn't in a great state and can be difficult to implement across all the browsers your application may support. In fact you may find you have to fall back to a JavaScript-based solution to drag and drop where the support is lacking.

However, native drag and drop, combined with newer APIs like the File API (out of scope of this book, but it allows the browser to read files without the server side) allows users to drag files straight into the browser. These kinds of features are appearing as beta features in applications such as Gmail, allowing users with browsers that support the bleeding edge drag and drop API, if there is such a thing, to experience the very latest technology.

You'll need to carefully weigh up whether native drag and drop is the right choice for your application.

CHAPTER 9

Geolocation

Remy Sharp

THE GEOLOCATION API is one of those APIs that has absolutely nothing to do with the HTML5 specification, and was created by the W3C rather than the WHATWG. In fact, it was never even part of the original Web Applications specification (though it does now reference the HMTL5 specification), but it's so darn cool that we had to include it in this book. In actuality, it's a key API when it comes to applications and adding some wicked—yes, wicked—social interaction.

The API is incredibly simple to work with, and you can easily enhance your web apps if they make use of any geo data by plugging this API into the app and saving your visitors from having to finger or scroll all over your map to find themselves.

Currently Firefox 3.5, Chrome 5, Safari 5 and Opera 10.60 all have support for the geolocation API—not a bad state to be in for a bleeding edge technology. In addition, a lot of new mobile phones and mobile browsers are supporting the geolocation API, particularly through the mobile WebKit implementation. Fennec, Mozilla's mobile browser also supports geolocation which might be used on the Android device for instance. In addition, if you're using the Open Web technologies to build your applications, PhoneGap, the framework for deploying Open Web mobile apps, provides the geolocation API.

Sticking a pin in your visitor

The geolocation API gives us a way to locate the exact position of our visitor. There are already lots of applications that make use of this API, ranging from mapping, as seen on Google Maps in **Figure 9.1**, to location-based social networks such as Gowalla and Google Buzz.

FIGURE 9.1 Google Maps detects geolocation support and adds the "locate me" functionality.

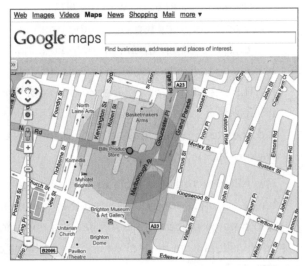

The geolocation API offers two methods for getting the geo information from your user:

1. getCurrentPosition is a one-shot method for grabbing the user's current location.

2. watchPosition keeps an eye on their position and keeps polling at regular intervals to see if their location has changed. watchPosition mirrors getCurrentPosition's functionality, but also if the user's position changes, it will tell your code.

Both getCurrentPosition and watchPosition work asynchronously to ascertain the user's location. There is one exception to that rule: if the user is visiting your site for the first time *and* the browser forces a model dialog asking for permission to share your location. When using either of these methods, most devices will prompt the user and ask whether they want to share their location with the application. If they don't agree to sharing their location, and you've told the geolocation API to pass errors to a specific function, it will be called with the error details.

The specification says:

> "User agents must not send location information to websites without the express permission of the user."

So it's up to the browser to prompt users to inform them that we're trying to grab their current position. Different browsers handle this in different ways. Firefox, for example, offers a non-modal, non-blocking alert asking users if they want to share their location (see **Figure 9.2**). This means your application continues to execute.

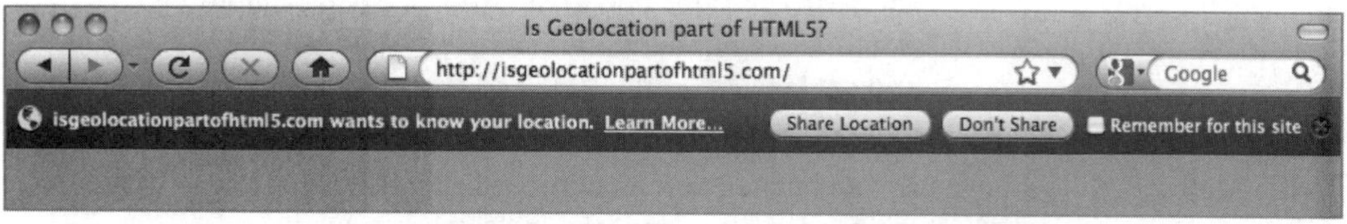

FIGURE 9.2 Firefox being asked to share the user's location.

Other browsers, such as Mobile Safari, prompt the user with a model dialog, stopping all code execution until the user responds (**Figure 9.3**).

FIGURE 9.3 Mobile Safari with a model dialog, blocking the app from continuing.

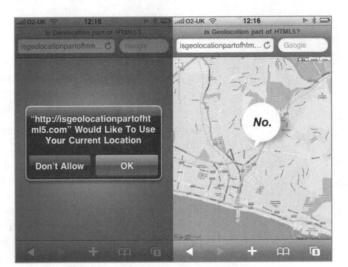

API methods

The geolocation API exists inside the navigator object and contains only three methods:

- getCurrentPosition
- watchPosition
- clearWatch

The watchPosition and clearWatch are paired methods. The watch and clear methods work the same way that setInterval and setTimeout work. watchPosition returns a unique identifier that is passed in to clearWatch to clear that particular watch.

As I mentioned before, both getCurrentPosition and watchPosition mirror each other and take the same arguments:

- success handler
- error handler
- geolocation options

Simple usage of the geolocation API would be to pass a success handler to the getCurrentPosition method:

```
navigator.geolocation.getCurrentPosition(function (position) {
  alert('We found you!');
  // now do something with the position data
});
```

Got you: the success handler

If the user permits the browser to share his geolocation and there's no other error, the success handler will be called, which is the first argument to getCurrentPosition and watchPosition.

The handler receives a Position object containing two properties: coords object (containing coordinate information) and a timestamp. The coordinates object is where the interesting stuff is sitting. There are really two grades of data in the position object. The first grade is appearing in all the browsers with geolocation support: Chrome 5, Firefox 3.5+, Mobile Safari & Safari 5, and Android 2.0:

- readonly attribute double latitude

- readonly attribute double longitude

- readonly attribute double accuracy

Note that accuracy is the measurement of the latitude and longitude accuracy in meters. You could use this to show a radius of accuracy if you were mapping the user's position.

The second grade of data inside the coordinates object are supported, but they currently don't have any values associated. They will be null, 0, or NaN in all the browsers currently supporting native geolocation:

- readonly attribute double altitude

- readonly attribute double altitudeAccuracy

- readonly attribute double heading

- readonly attribute double speed

Using the coordinate data, you could easily map the user's current position on something like a Google map:

```
if (navigator.geolocation) {
  navigator.geolocation.getCurrentPosition(function
  ¬ (position) {
    var coords = position.coords;
    showMap(coords.latitude, coords.longitude,
    ¬ coords.accuracy);
  });
}
```

In a lot of applications, it's likely that the user will be offered a manual way to set his current position. If the geolocation method is available, the site may offer the advanced functionality, progressively enhancing the page or the whole experience.

An example can be seen at **http://owlsnearyou.com**. Upon visiting the site, if geolocation is available, it reloads the page with your position loaded (see **Figure 9.4**), showing you where you can go owl hunting, if that's the activity that gets you going after a day of HTML5 development. If geolocation isn't available, it simply asks you to enter your location.

Geo 404: the error handler

The second argument to the `getCurrentPosition` and `watchPosition` method is the error handler. This is particularly important if you want to provide some alternative method of location (such as manually) or you want to notify the user of any errors in getting her position. The error handler may trigger if the user denies her position, but it could be that the user has given you permission and now you are watching her position on a mobile device and the phone has gone out of reception. This too would cause the error handler to trigger.

The error handler receives a single argument containing a position error object containing two properties:

- `readonly attribute unsigned short code`
- `readonly attribute DOMString message`

The code property will be only one of the following:

- PERMISSION_DENIED (numeric value 1)
- POSITION_UNAVAILABLE (numeric value 2)
- TIMEOUT (numeric value 3)

The message property is useful for developing and debugging but wouldn't be appropriate to show the user. The message property isn't always available (as it's not currently in Firefox 3.6+).

For example, if you used the following code and elected to not share the position, the page announces "Permission denied: means we can't determine your position."

```
if (navigator.geolocation) {
  navigator.geolocation.getCurrentPosition(function
  ¬(position) {
    var coords = position.coords;
    showMap(coords.latitude, coords.longitude,
    ¬coords.accuracy);
  }, function (error) {
    var errorTypes = {
      1: 'Permission denied',
      2: 'Position is not available',
      3: 'Request timeout'
    };

    alert(errorTypes[error.code] + ": means we can't
    ¬determine your position");
  });
}
```

The alternative error: on success

One alternative to the error handler is if the accuracy on the success call is a huge number. When I once visited a page that was supposed to detect my location, whilst working from home in Brighton on the south coast of England, the map placed me dead in the centre of London. When I checked under the hood using Firebug's console log I could see the accuracy of the geolocation request was set to 140,000 meters—that's about 90 miles of inaccuracy; as a radius that's pretty damn inaccurate! Understandable how the site wasn't sure exactly where I was. I would strongly recommend that while developing applications that use geolocation you also check the accuracy of the success call. If the accuracy is such a large value, it might be worth ignoring the data altogether and letting the users tell you their location manually.

Configuring the geolocation

Finally, the third argument to both getCurrentPosition and watchPosition are the geolocation options. All the geolocation options are *optional*, as you've seen, and are made up as follows:

- enableHighAccuracy (Boolean, default false)
- timeout (in milliseconds, default infinity/0)
- maximumAge (in milliseconds, default 0)

For example, to request high accuracy, a two-second timeout, and to never use old geo data, call getCurrentPosition using the following options (where success and error are predefined functions):

```
navigator.geolocation.getCurrentPosition(success, error, {
  enableHighAccuracy: true,
  timeout: 2000,
  maximumAge: 0
});
```

The enableHighAccuracy tells the device to try to get a more accurate reading on the latitude and longitude. On a mobile device, this may be to make use of the GPS on a phone, which could consume more power on the mobile device. Typically, you want the battery to last as long as possible, which is why by default, enableHighAccuracy is set to false.

The timeout tells the geolocation lookup how long it should wait before giving up and triggering the error handler (but won't start counting down if it's waiting for the user to approve the request). If it does timeout, the error code is set to 3 (TIMEOUT). Setting a zero time out (the current default) tells the browser to never time out.

Finally, maximumAge can be used to tell the browser whether to use recently cached position data. If there is a request that is within the maximumAge (in milliseconds), it is returned instead of requesting a new position. maximumAge can also be Infinity, which tells the browser to *always* use a cached position. Setting the maximumAge to zero (the default value) means the browser must look up a new position on each request.

How it works under the hood: it's magic

The geolocation API uses a few different techniques in acquiring your position. Most of it is black magic to most people, including myself, but it's worth having an idea about what's under the hood as it will affect the accuracy of the position data.

GPS is one of the obvious methods for getting position data. More computing devices are being fitted out with GPS, ranging from mobile phones to laptops. Assuming there's a clear enough line to the GPS ground station (which picks up readings from satellites to triangulate your position—yep, more black magic), then you'll have a very accurate reading on your position. GPS should also be able to give you altitude, which we saw in the second grade of properties in the coordinates object. So far this data isn't showing up in browsers, but I'd expect this to become available in time as mobile computing evolves quickly.

Another method would be using network information, which would be typical if used via a desktop browser such as Firefox. The network information could use wifi triangulation and IP addresses to make a best guess at your location. The developer makes a call to the browser's geolocation API, which in turn the browser makes a call to a third-party service such as Skyhook or Google. Although this may not be as accurate as GPS (meter-age-wise), it could make for a very good backup as GPS doesn't work very well indoors or in highrise urban locations.

Overall it's not terribly important to know what makes geolocation tick, but if you need to get the high accuracy you might want to be wary of using the more power-hungry devices such as GPS and be wary of killing your user's battery.

All in all, it's some very cool black magic.

Summary

In the UK, when red telephone boxes were still a common sight, inside each of these boxes included a printed note of the current address that you were calling from. This was so that if you had to call the police or an ambulance you knew where you were. Of course, this also helped after a hazy Friday night, calling home for a lift because you didn't know where you were.

Browsers now come shipped with this feature built in, and it's one of the simplest APIs available to implement. If your web site needs any location-based information from your user, then you can see it's easy as pie to progressively enhance your page to support this new API. It's only a matter of time until someone builds the web site that you open, and it instantly tells you your nearest greasy spoon cafe or curry house all entirely dependent on the current time and your current location.

CHAPTER 10

Messages, Workers, and Sockets

Remy Sharp

WEB MESSAGING, Web Workers, and Web Sockets are all different APIs but all have the same communication API, which is why I will show you all three together. Only the Messaging API is part of the official HTML5 spec, but all three of these APIs are valuable additions to any web application.

Messaging allows for sending messages from one domain to another, something that Ajax security policies have long prevented—for good reason—but is now starting to open up with the right security measurements in place.

> **NOTE** The new XML-
HttpRequest level 2 object
(http://www.w3.org/TR/XML-
HttpRequest2/), out of scope for
this book but already in WebKit
and Firefox, supports cross-
domain requests (with the right
level of server security). It also
includes progress events for
monitoring uploads.

Browsers are effectively *single threaded* applications, in that when JavaScript is running or perhaps being parsed, the page isn't rendering. Equally, when JavaScript is performing a long and complicated function, the whole browser can be seen to lock up. What Web Workers does is introduce a simplified idea of *threads* for browsers. A worker allows me to ring fence a particular block of code and it will run without affecting the browser at all, as if I have created a new thread of operation allowing the main browser thread to continue uninterrupted.

Finally, sockets are a way of creating a connected stream to your server (for server boffs out there: a TCP connection), and allows two-way real-time communication between the server and the client. The typically *hello world* app is a chat client, but the possibilities of use are endless. Sockets go a long way towards replacing Comet-based code. Comet uses a variety of techniques to achieve real-time streaming data from a server. Web Sockets simplify this process on the client side, as we'll see later in this chapter.

Chit chat with the Messaging API

I wanted to show you the Messaging API first because the next two APIs, Web Workers and Web Sockets, both use this common method of communication. So think of this as your gentle primer on communication.

The Messaging API has very good support across all browsers (yes, including IE) and offers a simple API for posting plain text messages from one origin (or domain, to you and me) to another. For example, if you want to send some information to a widget you have in an iframe, you can do it using the Messaging API. This will still work if the widget is on a completely different domain than the site hosting the iframe.

Sending messages across domains

If Bruce has a document that wants to communicate with my document, say either in an iframe or perhaps in a popup window, it needs a reference to the window object (of my document) and he can then call the postMessage method to pass some message to it. The JavaScript in Bruce's document will look like this:

```
var t = document.getElementsByTagName('iframe')[0];
t.contentWindow.postMessage('favourite instrument?',
¬ 'http://brucelawson.co.uk');
```

The target origin argument being passed to postMessage is required. This must match the origin of your contentWindow object (the target window, my document in this example) and it must be supplied. If the origins don't match, a security error will be thrown, stopping the script from continuing. If the origin isn't passed in, the JavaScript will throw a syntax error—not helpful, but something to watch out for if you forget. One last tip: Remember to wait for the target to finish loading. The target is still a document that needs to be parsed and loaded. If the browser hasn't loaded the document and you try to send it a message, the JavaScript will fail entirely with a similar syntax error.

My document is being referenced via an iframe on Bruce's page, and it contains the following JavaScript:

```
window.addEventListener('message', function (event) {
  if (event.data == 'favourite instrument?') {
    if (event.origin == 'http://remysharp.com') {
      event.source.postMessage('brand new clarinet',
      ¬ event.origin);
    } else if (event.origin == 'http://brucelaweson.co.uk') {
      event.source.postMessage('rusty old trombone',
      ¬ event.origin);
    }
  }
}, false);
```

> **NOTE** The previous code list uses **addEventListener** rather than **onmessage** because Firefox doesn't appear to respond to **onmessage** on the **window** object. This is best practice anyway, but it would mean we also need to hook IE using **attachEvent**, which I've not included in my example.

My script sets an event listener listening for messages being passed to the window. Inside the event object is a data property containing the message that was passed in. Along with the data property, there are a number of other useful properties sitting inside the event: origin and source.

The event.origin gives me the domain that the message came from. I can use this, as I have in the previous code listing, to determine whether I want to process the message. This is policy control at a very rudimentary level.

The event.source points back to the window object making the original call to my document, i.e., Bruce's document. This is useful to be able to communicate back and forth. Of course your onmessage event handler could do a lot more, like make an Ajax request to the server on the same domain.

What about sending more than strings?

In the examples I've shown you so far, I've only passed strings in messages back and forth. What about if you want to send more than just a string? What if you have an object with properties and values?

Well, the good news is the specification describes what's supposed to happen when a browser has to safely send data from one source to another. It describes how to clone the data and how it should be treated.

However ... most browsers don't support this process. In fact, most browsers simply coerce the object into a string. That sucks for you and me. It means that instead of the nicely constructed object, you'll get [object Object] in the event.data property. In fact, we saw this before in Chapter 6, "Data Storage," where we try to store objects in localStorage. So in the same way as we got around the issue with localStorage, you can use JSON.stringify to convert your JavaScript object into a string, pass it to postMessage and then, on the receiving side, convert it back to a native JavaScript object using JSON.parse.

Using JSON.stringify and JSON.parse will be useful methods for transferring more complicated objects from window to target, as we'll see in the next sections on Web Workers and Web Sockets.

Threading using Web Workers

Web Workers are part of a separate specification to the HTML5 spec, but are a key feature in building web applications.

A worker is a way of running a discrete block of JavaScript in a background process to the main browser. This is effectively a *thread*. What this means is the worker runs in the background without interfering with the main browser thread.

The browser is already responsible for requesting and parsing files, rendering the view, and executing JavaScript, and anything that consumes the browser's processing time causes all other jobs to wait. This is where Web Workers come to the rescue.

Why use a worker?

If you've ever written any dodgy JavaScript that goes haywire, causing your browser to start fuming like it's about to explode, then you have experienced the single-threadedness of browsers. Eventually, if the browser's smart, it'll give you the option to terminate the dodgy code, something like **Figure 10.1**.

FIGURE 10.1 Some browsers will interrupt JavaScript that's gone wild, and give you the option to nuke it into space.

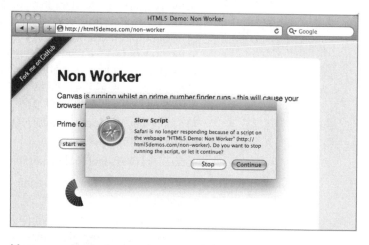

More worrying is the much more subtle issues. Say you've written the latest and greatest web application that does the most amazing photo manipulation. You're using all the *l33t* skills you learnt from this book—canvas, storage, offline applications—but when it comes to adding a photo filter, it takes 30 seconds. It's not the 30 seconds that's the problem; it's the fact they can't do *anything* in the browser for those 30 seconds. What if your user changed her mind and wanted to cancel the filter? Obviously a situation you want to avoid.

This scenario is perfect for a Web Worker because the entire filter processing can happen in the background, and the main browsing window is left alone to continue to be responsive to your visitor's requests.

Creating and working with workers

You can test for Web Worker support by checking whether the object is undefined:

```
if (typeof Worker != "undefined") {
  // do the jazzy stuff
}
```

Now that we know we've got support (Safari, Chrome, Opera, and Firefox currently support Web Workers) we can go about creating a new worker:

```
var worker = new Worker('my_worker.js');
```

A new worker object is fired up, reads in the my_worker.js JavaScript file and is now happily running and ready to be used. At this point, you'd be forgiven for thinking that you can call methods inside the worker from your document, and in fact that data can be returned from the worker to your document. Poppycock! No, in fact to work with a worker, everything must be communicated through posting messages between the worker and your document. Like some scene from *Romeo and Juliet*, exchanging letters of love between the browser and the worker.

The *only* way you get can information to the worker is via postMessage:

```
worker.postMessage('hello worker!');
```

The only way you can receive information from the worker is via the onmessage event handler:

```
worker.onmessage = function (event) {
  alert('The worker just sent me this: ' + event.data);
};
```

You should now be recognising the postMessage/onmessage combination from the Messaging API from earlier in this chapter. You remember how we can only send and receive strings in the Message API? You won't be surprised to know, then, that the Web Workers have the same constraint.

Equally, the code *inside* the worker must also communicate using the postMessage/onmessage combo. However a Web Worker doesn't have the same access as your normal document: It's very much sandboxed in and has access to only a select few APIs and functions, as I'll show you in the next section.

The only other method available to you via the worker object is terminate, which does exactly what it says on the tin. The worker ceases to run and worker object becomes limp and useless. In particular, you can't resume the worker; you'd have to create a brand new one.

> **NOTE** A slight caveat: Web Workers are supposed to be able to send objects, just as the Messaging API is, but most browsers coerce the object to a string. However, Firefox has implemented internal JSON.stringify/JSON.parse behind the scenes of sending and receiving messages to and from workers so you don't have to. So there's hope if the other browsers follow suit and allow us to send object through the messaging system.

What you can do inside a worker

Within a Web Worker you don't have access to such pleasures as the DOM. In fact, if you need to do anything with the DOM, you're going to have to *prepare* the work in the worker, then pass it to the parent document to do the actual DOM manipulation.

> **NOTE** Currently there are no Web Worker implementations that support accessing Web SQL Databases, though there are fixes in the works.

However there are a number of things you can do in a worker (according to the specification):

- `postMessage` and listen for inbound messages via `onmessage`
- `close`, to end the current worker
- Set event listeners
- `XMLHttpRequest`, for Ajax requests
- Timers, such as `setTimeout`, `setInterval`, and their clearing counterparts
- All the core JavaScript functions: `eval`, `isNaN`, `escape`, etc.
- Location object, the href of the worker script
- Web Sockets (which we'll discuss in the final section of this chapter)
- Web SQL Databases
- Web Workers
- `importScripts`

The following code is all I need in `my_worker.js` to communicate with the document from the earlier code listing:

```
onmessage = function (event) {
  if (event.data == "hello worker!") {
    postMessage("hello there, right back at you");
  } else {
    postMessage("Can't you see I'm busy, leave me alone");
  }
};
```

It's useful to know that, in a normal document, the this keyword would refer to the global scope, the window object. Here in the worker, the global scope is the worker instance. It also means that the this keyword inside of setTimeout and setInterval is he worker instance (where this would otherwise be the window object).

In these examples so far, our worker hasn't done anything particularly special. How about a worker that searches for prime numbers? This requires a super tight loop in JavaScript constantly spinning around looking for values that match a prime. All this and at the same time allowing your visitor to draw on a canvas while your app searches for prime numbers? Perhaps a strange use case, but we have workers to come to your rescue.

The main document will handle starting the worker and drawing on the canvas. The only code that's offloaded to the worker is the prime number searching.

```
var worker = new Worker('prime.js'),
    prime = document.getElementById('prime');
worker.onmessage = function(event) {
  prime.innerHTML = event.data;
};
```

The page continues to handle mousedown, move, and up events to draw on a canvas on the page. Inside the prime.js script we have:

```
onmessage = function (event) {
  // doesn't matter what the message is, just start the job
  run();
};

function run() {
  var n = 1;
  search: while (true) {
    n += 1;
    for (var i = 2; i <= Math.sqrt(n); i += 1)
      if (n % i == 0)
        continue search;
    // found a prime!
    postMessage(n);
  }
}
```

When the prime.js worker receives any message, it starts the prime number search. When you run this prime number drawing extravaganza of an application, everything runs smoothly, and you're able to create your perfect work of art whilst also searching for primes as seen in **Figure 10.2**.

Matryoshka dolls: workers inside workers

If you had a watchful eye, you would have spotted that from *within* a worker you can also create new workers. Currently only Firefox supports this, but it's part of the spec, so you should expect that other browsers will update to include this feature.

What this means is that you could spawn one worker, who then goes and splits its job into lots of delegated little jobs and passes them to sub-workers. Let's go back to the example of applying a complex filter to a photo in your super-sexy online image web app. To speed up the processing of the image—and if it made sense in the filter—you could split the image up into regions and pass each region of image data to a sub-worker.

As each worker returns, you reduce the pending count and once all the workers have finished, the main worker returns the final processed image data to the parent document. Something like this (I've left out some functions from the listing as this is just to demonstrate the idea):

```
var pendingWorkers = 0,
    results = {},
    workingWidth = 100;

onmessage = function (event) {
```

```
    var imageData = JSON.parse(event.data),
        worker = null;

    pendingWorkers = getNumberOfWorkers(imageData.width
    ¬/ workingWidth);
    // reset any old results
    results = {};

    for (var i = 0; i < pendingWorkers; i++) {
      worker = new Worker('photofilter.js');
      worker.postMessage(JSON.stringify({
        imageData: imageData,
        x: i * workingWidth,
        width: workingWidth
      }));
      worker.onmessage = storeResult;
    }
};

function storeResult(event) {
  var result = JSON.parse(event.data);

  buildUpImageData(result);

  pendingWorkers--;
  if (pendingWorkers <= 0) {
    postMessage(JSON.stringify(results));
  }
}
```

When the message is received from the sub-worker, the main worker above decreases the number of outstanding sub-workers. Once all the sub-workers have returned their slice of the image data, the final result is returned to the parent document.

The sub-worker, photofilter.js worker, would contain the following code to handle processing just a small region of the image data:

```
onmessage = function (event) {
  var data = JSON.parse(event.data);

  // perform some amazing feat of image processing
  var imageData = amazingImageProcess(data.imageData,
  ¬ data.x, data.width);
  postMessage(JSON.stringify({
```

```
    imageData: imageData,
    x: data.x
}));

// self close
close();
};
```

Notice also how photofilter.js, once it's done performing its task, calls the close() method. This allows the worker to terminate, since it's not required for use again.

Importing scripts and libraries to your worker

Web Workers is very much about modularising a block of code or functionality and running it in a stand-alone environment (that is, the worker itself). Web Workers can also load external JavaScript files and libraries via the importScripts method.

This is one of the few worker-specific methods. It accepts a list of URLs and loads them into the worker synchronously. You can load one script at a time, or you can load multiple scripts from within the worker:

```
importScripts('xhr.js');
importScripts('prime.js', 'number_crunch.js',
¬ 'captain_crunch.js');
```

Each script is processed one at a time. The script must be on the same origin as the worker—the same domain, cname, etc. The worker then synchronously loads the JavaScript into itself, returning to continue only once the script has finished processing.

Sharing a load with SharedWorkers

Another type of Web Worker is the SharedWorker, currently only supported in Chrome and WebKit (rather than Safari). A shared worker is pretty much like an average Web Worker except that multiple documents can access the same single instance of the worker. So this means that if you have several popups or several iframes, all of those documents can access this single shared worker and this single shared worker will serve all of those documents.

This would be useful for applications, for example, like Gmail or Facebook, where there may be some client-side data that needs to be maintained, such as the messages for the user, and you have several different windows open.

The worker can access and manage the website's client-side Web SQL Databases (discussed in Chapter 6) and it can also maintain the connection with the server, handling all the data that's coming in and out or even via a Web Socket to the server so that data is handled in real-time. The shared worker can then maintain all of the changes to the client-side messages database and then push all of those updates via postMessage to each of the popups, iframes, and so on.

This means that there's no getting data out of sync or race conditions if each of the popups, iframes, etc. was individually connecting to the server and trying to each manage the client side, since the shared worker is the single point of contact for all of that type of work.

The SharedWorker works very slightly differently when it comes to communication. For starters there's the concept of ports—this is an array-like object that contains a reference to each of the communication channels the shared worker has. Also, if you bind to the message event using addEventListener, you have to manually start the worker, which I'll show you in the following code sample.

In addition, within the worker the connect event fires when the SharedWorker is created, which can be used to keep track of how many connections the worker has to other documents.

The documents creating the SharedWorker contain the following code:

```
var worker = new SharedWorker('messages.js');
worker.port.addEventListener('message', function(event) {
  var messages = JSON.parse(event.data);
  showNewMessages(messages);
}, false);
worker.port.start();
```

In the previous example, you can see we're accessing the worker via the port property. This is how you interact and, in fact, distinguish between shared and nonshared workers. As the example binds to the message event using addEventListener, the worker must be connected manually using the .start()

method. The code wouldn't need this if it used onmessage. Next is the messages.js worker:

```
importScripts('xhr.js');
importScripts('database.js');

var connections = [];

onconnect = function(event) {
  connections.push(event.ports[0]);
}

var xhr = new XHR('/get-new-messages');
xhr.oncomplete = function (messages) {
  database.updateMessages(messages);

  for (var i = 0; i < connections.length; i++) {
    connections[i].postMessage(JSON.stringify(messages));
  }

  xhr.send(); // causes us to loop forever
};
xhr.send();
```

When a client document connects to the worker, the connect event is fired, which allows me to capture the connection port. This is collected through the event.ports[0] reference, even though there will never be more than one item inside the ports property. However the worker reference is inside this, so we can use this to post messages and receive messages.

As you see in the previous example, when the Ajax complete function runs, I loop through all of the connected ports and send them each a message of the new email messages that have come in. This way the connected clients act as dumb terminals, oblivious to any of the real work going on to store the messages in the client-side database.

Debugging a worker

We've gotten to the point in web development where the tools for debugging are so much better than 10 years ago. All the latest browsers come with their own JavaScript debugger (though Firefox still requires Firebug as a plugin); it's a haven of debugging when compared to the bad old days of using alert boxes left, right, and centre.

✳ **TIP** Chrome recently added a way to allow you to debug workers from the script tab in their Web Inspector, but what it's really doing is running the worker scripts through iframes; this does mean the console.log lines actually appear in the console. Very useful for debugging a closed black box!

Since now, with a Web Worker, you're working in a sandboxed environment, there is no access to the console debuggers. There's no native way to do console.log("who's the daddy?") in a worker. To compound this hurdle, there's not even an alert box we can use.

To debug a Web Worker, you may have to make up your own debugging methods.

Since you can move messages back and forth to the parent document, you can create some system for posting messages that should be sent to the console log. However with that, you need to create a system that doesn't just process strings, you need to have some agreed language between your workers and your main document, and this will depend entirely on your application. For instance, you could prefix debug messages with the keyword "log:"

```
importScripts('xhr.js');

var xhr = new XHR('/someurl');
xhr.oncomplete = function (data) {
  log('data contains ' + data.length + ' items');
};
xhr.send();


function log(msg) {
  postMessage('log ' + msg);
}
```

Note that xhr.js is my made-up XMLHttpRequest script that returns me some JSON data—you'll have to make your own!

In the main page in the onmessage event, I'll be looking for prefixes in messages and actioning them:

```
var worker = new Worker('xhr_thang.js');
worker.onmessage = function (event) {
  var data = event.data.split(' '),
      action = data.shift(), // grab the first word
      msg = data.join(' '); // put the message back together

  if (action == 'log') {
    console.log(msg);
  } else {
    // some other action
  }
};
```

> **NOTE** It's possible for a worker to get aborted or terminated through a method unknown to your code. If your worker is being killed off by the browser for some reason, then the `worker.onerror` event is going to fire. If you're closing the worker manually, you're having to do this from within the worker via `.close()` so you have the opportunity to notify the connected documents that your worker is closing.

In this example, my agreed grammar is all messages are prefixed with an action. This could be log, set, run, etc. What's important is I now have a way to inspect data that's inside the worker by sending data to my log function.

It's also useful to be able to poke around inside a worker, something I've found to be exceptionally useful when experimenting in JavaScript. In a non-worker environment, I can pop open my console of choice (Firebug, Dragonfly, etc.,) and from within there, I would log out and inspect all the properties on the `window` object, the `document`, then their properties, just to see what's supported and what I can play with. Since a worker is a closed environment, I would need to do this manually. So one of the online examples for this book includes a console that allows you to inspect a Web Worker and test code inside the worker and see what it produces. You can see the worker console at **http://introducinghtml5.com/examples/ch10/echo.html** (**Figure 10.3**).

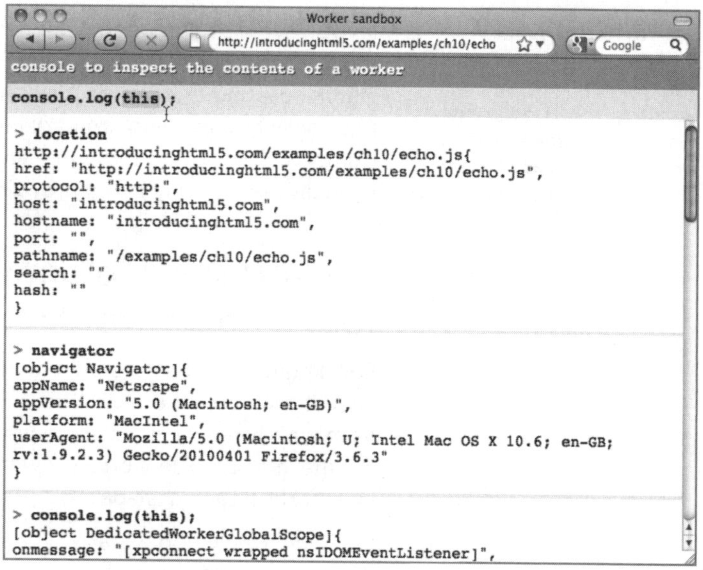

FIGURE 10.3 A demo console to inspect inside a Web Worker.

Web Sockets: working with streaming data

Web Sockets are one of the shiniest new APIs outside of the realm of HTML5, but they're actually really important for some of the real-time-based web applications that have emerged in recent times.

Web Sockets give you a *bi-directional* connection between your server and the client, the browser. This connection is also real-time and is permanently open until explicitly closed. This means that when the server wants to send your client something, that message is pushed to your browser immediately.

This is what Comet was aiming to achieve, and succeeding. Comet is a way of creating a real-time connection to your server, but it would do it using a variety of different hacks. Ultimately, if none of these hacks work, it would eventually fall back down to Ajax polling, which would constantly hit your server and that doesn't scale up very well.

> **NOTE** If the browser doesn't natively support Web Sockets, there's always a way using Flash. Hiroshi Ichikawa has written a Flash-based shim for Web Sockets that's available here: **http://github.com/gimite/ web-socket-js**.

If you have a socket open, your server can push data to all those connected sockets, and the server doesn't have to constantly respond to inbound Ajax requests. This is the move from polling to pushing, from reactive to proactive. This is what Comet was achieving through hacks, and this is what Web Sockets achieves natively in the browser.

Sockets solve latency of real-time applications

Low latency is a massive benefit of Web Sockets. Since your socket is always open and listening, as soon as data is pushed from the server, it just has to make its way to your browser, making the latency exceptionally low in comparison to something like an XMLHttpRequest-based Ajax request.

In theory, with Google Wave, if you have lots of people all in the same document, and you're all typing, you want to send all those keystrokes to all the connected people as soon as they happen. However, if you're using vanilla Ajax to do that, you would have to create a new XHR object every time a key is hit, and every one of those requests will contain all the headers that are sent with a normal XHR request, like the user agent string, the referrer URL, the accepted content type, and so on. All of this data for what was essentially only a keypress.

Whereas with sockets, because the connection is always open, all you need to send is the keystroke, which would then be disseminated to all the connected clients via the server, and *only* that keystroke would be sent.

The data sent has gone from Ajax, which will be perhaps 200–300 bytes of data, to a socket connection, which will be just a few bytes of data, perhaps around 10–20 bytes, which will be much more responsive and faster to transfer around the connected sessions.

The simple Web Socket API

The Web Socket API is also exceptionally easy to work with. Currently browsers only support sending strings (with the exception of Firefox and Web Workers), which we've seen with the Messaging API and Web Workers using postMessage and onmessage. Sockets work almost exactly the same.

This means that you can't (currently) send binary data—but I'd argue that in the web world we're used to working with JSON and it's not particularly a big deal to encode to JSON as the messages come in from a socket since we're already doing it for JSON Ajax requests.

The API is limited down to creating the connection, sending data down the socket, receiving and closing the socket. There's also an error handler and a state flag, for connecting, open, closing, and closed. Once you've closed the socket, the socket is completely closed down and can't be reopened. So if you need to reopen it, you need to create a new socket to go out.

Creating a new Web Socket is easy, and very much like a Web Worker. The protocol of the URL must be ws:// but the rest of the URL can be structured just as you would a normal URL to be:

```
var socket = new WebSocket('ws://myserver.com/tweets:8080/');
```

For this example, I'm only going to be listening to the messages that come from the tweets URL. Each is a new tweet from Twitter that my server has been set up to listen for (**Figure 10.4**).

> **NOTE** Regarding the ws:// server protocol: Writing about how to set up the server side is beyond the scope of this book, but there are already several libraries out in the wild that can add the Web Socket protocol. Using servers like Node.js I was able to get a Web Socket server up and running in around 20 minutes and documented it online: **http://remysharp.com/slicehost-nodejs-websockets/**.

FIGURE 10.4 A streaming connection showing tweets that my server was listening for.

The messages from the server are being delivered as JSON messages, forwarded on from Twitter's streaming API. So when they come in, I'll convert the JSON to data and render the tweet on the screen:

```
socket.onmessage = function(event) {
  var tweetNode = renderTweet(JSON.parse(event.data));
  document.getElementById('tweets').appendChild(tweetNode);
};
```

Now in as many as four lines of JavaScript (excluding the renderTweet function), I've got streaming real-time tweets on my page.

Doing more than listening with a socket

As I said before, there are more methods available on a socket over just listening. Since *chat* is the *hello world* of Comet, I felt it only fair to show you a simple example of what chat would look like using Web Sockets:

```javascript
var socket = new WebSocket("ws://my-chat-server.com:8080/"),
    me = getUsername();

socket.onmessage = function(event) {
  var data = JSON.parse(event.data);
  if (data.action == 'joined') {
    initiliseChat();
  } else {
    showNewMessage(data.who, data.text);
  }
};

socket.onclose = function () {
  socket.send(JSON.stringify({
    action: 'logoff',
    username: me
  }));
  showDisconnectMsg();
};

socket.onopen = function() {
  socket.send(JSON.stringify({
    action: 'join',
    username: me
  }));
};
```

This simple pseudo code shows you how the same techniques we used in the Message API can help to get around the limitations of plain text. The Web Sockets API really is as simple as that. All the negotiation is done out of sight by the browser for you; all the buffering is done for you (though you can check the current bufferedAmount on the socket). In fact, the communication process is even easier than setting up an XHR object!

Summary

This final chapter has equipped you with the last of your HTML5 web application armory. You can now create multi-threaded, multi-window, cross-domain, low-latency, real-time thingymegiggies using the simplest of string-based communication methods. Now go build something awesome.

And finally...

Hopefully, you've been enlightened by our brief foray into the new structures and APIs that you can use.

There are loads more cool stuff in the spec that we haven't shown you because it's not implemented yet. For example, you can register the browser as a content handler so that clicking a document or photo or video on your desktop opens the browser and goes to a web application that can edit that document, complete with application toolbars, all built with HTML5. But it's still awaiting implementation.

Forget the marketing B.S. of "Web 2.0." We're at the beginning of Web *Development* 2.0: powerful languages like HTML5, SVG, and CSS3 will revolutionise the way we build the Web. Browsers support more and more of these aspects of these languages (and you can be certain that more and more support is being added daily).

Have a play with the new features. Experiment with the new markup structures, manipulate video on the fly, and build fun and attractive games and apps that use <canvas>. By reading this book, you're demonstrating that you're an early adopter, ahead-of-the-curve, so please set a good example to your colleagues; respect those visitors to your new creations who have older browsers or assistive technologies.

Thanks for buying this book and sticking with us. See you around. All the code (and more) is available at www.introducinghtml5.com. Bon voyage: enjoy building incredible things. kthxbai.

—Bruce Lawson and Remy Sharp
Bali, Birmingham, and Brighton, Nov 09–May 10

INDEX

A

\<a\> element, 54
accessibility. *See also* WAI-ARIA
  canvas element, 139
  dragging and dropping, 184–185
  multimedia, 110–113
  outlining algorithm, 36–37
Accessible Rich Internet Applications. *See* WAI-ARIA
addEventListener method, 106–110, 199, 208
\<address\> element, 58
animating paintings, 134–137
APIs, retained-mode *versus* immediate mode, 124
\<applet\> element, 60
ARIA (Accessible Rich Internet Applications).
    See WAI-ARIA
aria-* attribute, 63
aria-grabbed attribute, 185
aria-required attribute, 76
aria-valuenow attribute, 81–82
\<article\> element, 20–21, 37–42, 52, 54, 58, 111
  block-level links, 38
  comments as nested articles, 29–30
Asian languages, 55
\<aside\> element, 17, 19–20, 33, 52, 54
attributes attribute, 63
Audacity software, 101
\<audio\> element, 54, 94, 96, 99–100
autocomplete attribute, 74, 78
autofocus attribute, 75
autoplay attribute, 95

B

\<b\> element, 59
Baranovskiy, Dmitry, 124
base64 encoded assets, 133
beginPath method, 122–123
\<big\> element, 60
object\> element, 92–93
\<blink\> element, 60
block-level elements, 38, 54
\<blockquote\> element, 28, 34–35
\<body\> element, 3–4, 5, 27–28, 34
boldface, \<b\> element, 59
bug reports, 12
\<button\> element, 54, 68

C

Camen, Kroc, 100
cancelEvent function, 179
canplaythrough and canplay events, 108
canPlayType method, 102–103
\<canvas\> element/canvases, 54
  accessibility, 139
  animating paintings, 134–137
  basics, 118–119
  capturing images, 126–129
  data URLs, saving to, 132–133
  drawing applications, 115–116
  drawing state, 137
  fill styles, gradients and patterns, 118–122
  Harmony application, 115, 117
  MS Paint replication, 115–116
  paths, 122–124
  pixels, pushing, 130–132
  rectangles, 118
    gradients and patterns, 118–120
  rendering text, 138–139
  resizing canvases, 122
  transformation methods, 124–126
case sensitivity, pattern attribute, 78
\<center\> element, 60
character encoding, UTF-8, 2
charset="utf-8" attribute, XHTML and XML *versus* HTML5, 2
checkValidity attribute, 86
checkValidity method, 85–86
Chisholm, Wendy, 51
cite attribute, 28
\<cite\> element, 58
classes
  attributes, 6, 8
  names, Google index research, 6
clear attribute, 147
clearInterval method, 127
clearRect method, 125
clearWatch method, 190
codecs, 98–99
color input type, 74
Comet, 212, 215
\<command\> element, 62, 65
comments as nested articles, 29–30